THE SOUND OF VIOLENCE

STU ALLEN

ISBN:9798373172073

CONTENTS

FOREWORDS

My guess is that you have come to this book having already read "Simply the Beast". If you haven't then you have missed out on a story that tells of my old business partner, Stu Allen's, unfathomable love for 18th century French novelist Gabrielle-Suzanne de Villeneuve's most famous fairy tale and a Bonnie Tyler song most famously covered by Tina Turner in 1989. I've lost you, haven't I?

Well, if you had bothered to read Stu's first book you might be thinking you had lost me quite a while back. After all, we ceased running Extreme Entertainment in 2003 together after we closed the doors on The Combat Performance Academy and we hadn't produced a show since 2001. Let's just say, that any actor playing my part – don't say " a young Ben Stiller" you bastards – in a biopic adaptation of "Simply the Beast" would be a bit pissed off at how little script was allocated to him after act one. Okay, I hear you saying that this isn't about me but to paraphrase a line Stu used to love spoken by a certain said young actor in one of his better roles: "I have the page and you don't so you will read every damn word I have to say!"

Still here? Stu has you well trained... or is that traumatised?

Anyway, my life was taking me in a different direction. I was in the thick of writing my first book connected to all that circus culture Stu will have told you about and also getting back into my martial arts education, plus I was flying the nest in Oxfordshire and moving in with my future wife in Warwickshire. As it turned out, the day after Stu first invited me back in a guest appearance in the second incarnation of Extreme World Warfare I proposed to her. I eventually returned with my family to the former Chipperfield's Farm to build our house next door to my mum's home and the zoo she had built with my dad. However, by then Stu had also flown the nest with his wife, Tarnya, to live in Hastings and his parents had followed him!

Just looking back at that last paragraph makes me think of the contrasts in Stu I could relate to when we first began working together. As you will read in the latest volume of his life, unpredictability was something Stu enjoyed. Even during The Dominator's earliest days, the character was constantly changing and never conforming to what might be expected. This was always the case with EWW.

And so it follows with this book. Stu is quick to bounce off from a depressive sounding dirge condemning the mediocrity of the 2010s' wrestling scene to a joyous celebration of good people he has known. A chapter dedicated to the one and only Jerry was certainly in order, and this includes Stu's early friendship with King Wes's soul mate, the irreplaceable Ginny. As the book moves through the personal troubles my old friend faced, it's worth understanding what a truly important force for good these two were in his life. From the moment Stu introduced me to them on a totally silly EWW bargain boat ride with third promoter Josh at the wheel, I felt the infectious happiness they brought to any situation.

Since Stu has been at Hastings, I watched from afar at how EWW changed. Here and there Stu would share something with me that he thought I would enjoy, and sometimes something else would arrive via my social media platform. From 2012 onwards I could see that the promotion was coming the closest to Stu's vision. The Extreme Academy was third time lucky for Stu as far as running his own wrestling school goes. With the support of his wife, Tarnya 'Skarlett' Allen, who was also his most dedicated pupil and clearly a wrestling star in high ascent, EWW finally had its own complete roster of home grown talent. This provided the solid base of loyalty the earlier incarnations of the promotion sorely lacked. Now the show could be a truly united front.

From this moment onwards EWW progressed in the right direction with a sizeable local fan base, a great venue and everyone on board understanding that the show needed to be the star. I recall when Stu invited me to perform a guest spot to be The Spirit of Instinct one last time in a Faustian pact angle with Skarlet, he was keen then to show me how ideas we had only dreamed about achieving were becoming a reality. Yes, the slicker promos and better produced videos created by technological whizzes who had been child EWW fans in our day are wonderful, but the clear point he wanted to make then was how the stories could breathe.

Now, he wasn't having to constantly to load all this stuff into programmes that people didn't read or work them in turn of the 21st century discussion forums before having to readapt everything just before or on the night of the show because of unreliable freelance wrestlers. This time he could have the soap opera and build the audience psychology. He could take his time by spoon-feeding material on social media and from show to show. Characters could develop and storylines could continue.

Perhaps EWW might be seen as the reactionary now, given the minimalist approach adopted by the newer age of wrestling, but I still see the same uncompromising spirit. The defiance now is to embrace the spectacle and to defy the blandness of workers in black trunks. Who would have thought the struggle would be to continue presenting engaging shows with personalities that inspire emotional investment. Mind you, I saw the same thing happen in circus as colourful variety and diversity was forced to make way for faceless uniformity.

Having said that, as Stu tells us in this volume, there's plenty to still fight in the legacy of the old guard. This book, more than the previous volume, delves into the abuses committed against workers in professional wrestling subculture. This is where we find the real darkness.

During EWW's early days Stu once said to me, 'One of the scariest things in life is when you discover adults are just big kids'. Therefore, if part one of the Stu Allen story is concerned about conveying that punkish ambition from its childish desire for anarchy to shake up the pro wrestling scene followed by an adolescent angst of having to deal with life's cruel realities, then part two is about managing those realities as only a middle-aged Dominator can. Stu is at his most reflective in this volume as he looks at a changing era and then at big changes he is trying make. The book resumes his story by becoming selective over his worked fights in this new time. By contrast, it ends by his choosing what real issues are worth fighting.

- **Jamie Clubb 2022**

I first saw Stu 'The Dominator' Allen when he appeared on 'Jerry Springer UK' together with Alex Shane... I had already been a fan of wrestling for years and had recently discovered that there was an independent scene in England, but hadn't yet found a way in.
Stu and Alex came on stage in full gear- Stu of course with the spiked shoulder pads and face paint. Probably the thing I have always loved most about wrestling was the

larger-than-life characters it presents us with- and Stu certainly fit that description. I immediately thought: that's it, I need to get involved!

Very shortly after that I found a wrestling school and started training.
I knew that Stu ran EWW and had seen the posters and some articles about the shows he put on... it was a secret hope of mine that I would one day perform there. Several years later I go the opportunity- Stu booked me for my first EWW match. It was a pivotal moment for me, despite the fact that at this point I had been already quite successful on the British wrestling scene, working for Hammerlock (NWA-UK) and then FWA, another cutting-edge promotion with Alex Shane as the figure head.

EWW was not just a bucket list check. Stu let me really be myself- I worked as a heel for the first time within the UK and got to cut a promo, which was a rare treat for me. And more than that - well, you know they say never meet your heroes - but this experience was the opposite.
The truth is, if it hadn't been for Stu appearing on my TV screen several years earlier to promote his company, I probably would never have pursued this wrestling dream that became my life and gave me so much. In addition, it was a joy to find that Stu was not only a spectacular performer and promoter, but a kind, generous, respectful gem of a person that I am incredibly grateful to have met and worked with. Stu is inextricably linked to my wrestling career and remains a friend to this day.

- **Katarina Waters (Katie Lee Burchill WWE)**

Making meaningful impressions in an outlandish industry such as Professional Wrestling, with its countless bizarre and over-the-top personalities, is not a simple task to explain.

The reasoning behind how the author of this book made such impressions upon me over the years, is however rather straightforward.
It all comes down to consistency. Stuart Allen is the finest example of a consistent Professional Wrestler that you're ever likely to find. In both his mind and method.

My own and Stu Allens' beginnings in Professional Wrestling are not that dissimilar. We began our journeys around the same time, albeit on different continents, and shared long-since defunct experiences that came with being introduced to the Professional Wrestling business at that time. It was a hardening process that tested dreams in ways that only veteran wrestlers who are still involved with the current scene today are fully able to appreciate. The present route to the inside of the wrestling business has changed. Yet, as relatively easy as it might be nowadays to call yourself a wrestler, many of these guys and girls are in incredible shape. They visually put the majority of my generation to shame when we were at their stage of the game.

Hands up, along our travels, myself and Stu both got to witness and even partook in certain shady aspects that came along with the nastier side of our industry. (Some of those things may or may not even get a mention in this very book, so I won't open up any cans of worms here.) Suffice to say, that our ideas of what life was going to be like inside of Professional Wrestling, were abruptly altered, very soon after entering it.

I've said many times before, Stu Allen, or, 'The Dominator', brought a much-needed legitimate face to Professional Wrestling in the UK.
During a time that the average British 'new school' wrestler might have only been in their early to mid-teenage years, possessed little to no physical presence, and even less knowledge of what a combat situation ought to look like, Stu would regularly and unabashedly, be heard admonishing entire locker rooms over just how disgraceful he thought they were for not making enough effort to make themselves look like wrestlers, and instead selfishly chose to make a business that was already floundering, look even more of a joke by agreeing to be placed in a position where they are performing in front of paying audiences when they were not ready.

Now, whether in full 'Dominator' apparel, or standing un-gimmicked in his street clothing, a Stuart Allen reprimand can be pretty intimidating. But secretly, I think that he knew, that the faces he was addressing, knew themselves, that hitting the weights wasn't a necessary investment for them to get booked, so why should they? The real fault lay at the feet of the promoters for not being demanding enough of their talent. So of course, this would lead to Stu frequently being seen confronting promoters about his concerns also. You see...Consistent. In mind and method.

Legitimacy, or a lack thereof, has been a bugbear of Stu's for as long as I've known him. It is something that he takes very seriously and insists upon others doing the same. In his own gym, if you turn up unprepared to improve physically, thinking that you'll just addle along to get by, I'll personally wager that you won't be returning with the same mindset..if you can return at all that is.

Stu Allen is an unsung advocate for the survival of Professional Wrestling in the UK. And it is of the highest honour that he selected me to supply a foreword for his second book.

- **Justin Richards**

CHAPTER ONE
UNTO THE BREACH

Once more unto the breach dear friends, once more. Thanks so much for coming back for round two.

For those of you who are new to my world, firstly I'd invite you to read my first tome, Simply the Beast, and catch yourself up. That was my introduction not just into the world, but a filthy world of sub culture show business packed out with heroes, villains and everything in between and how me and a group of three friends built our own empire to strengthen the industry we loved and to help stamp out some of the bad element that were creeping in, in a time when pro wrestling was as flat as a fart in church, and we were a main part of the glue that held it together. In a nutshell, that's what we did. After wrestling under many different names across Europe, cutting my teeth against veterans who would sooner spit in my eye than shake my hand, I finally found my footing with a gimmick and look that would go on to serve me well for another two decades as The Dominator - The British Beast.

In that time I travelled the world and thanks to wrestling got paid to visit many places I'd very possibly never had the opportunity to have seen otherwise and make many lifelong friends around the world whilst doing it, both comrades and fans alike. We changed the entire EWW backstage team and recruited a booking and safeguarding team that I will talk about later. Our kids from our Extreme Academy of wrestling grew from strength to strength and became huge parts of our shows.

As I begin writing this second book, we are in much the same position now as we were when I took up the challenge of writing Simply the Beast. As I write this, we are about to come out of the second Lockdown and into a three-tier system which has left most of the country baffled. Phrases like 'the new normal' and 'social distancing' have been rushed into our everyday speech unlike anything else in existence. Thanks to the media, people are clambering over themselves to be afraid, I don't recognise the country or the people in it. There is tribalism everywhere and people have developed a kind of Stockholm Syndrome fondness and equal fear of it all, usually to whichever suits their narrative We have seen the rise in the cult of fake news thanks to old President Trump. A legitimate questioning of the unscrupulous media but done by an equally unscrupulous 'politician'. He single handedly used the cult of personality to maximum effect and gave credence to the Q Anon brigade. A highly triggered cult of their own who alarmingly think that 'evidence' of such things as Princess Diana's faked death and satanic paedophilic groups and secret tunnels is widely available on, wait for it......YouTube.

When questioned they either meet you with self-satisfied grins on their faces, as if they are party to some special information the rest of us don't know about, or get hostile very fucking quickly. It's opium for red necks.
I have to say as soon as I hear people talking about 'They' I immediately switch off. That's when you know the conversation is beyond repair. 'They'. So invested are these folk in the Illuminati and the Rothschilds that 'They' is now good enough to encompass everything.

Having said that, it makes life a little bit more interesting thinking that everything has all been planned. The thought that things sometimes just happen is never up for debate as it tears a hole in the entire thing. Chaos is frightening. Conspiracy is comforting. But I'm not one for the cancel culture of censorship, far from it, so let's all discuss it. I'm pro debate. Mass debate you might say....

My podcast Stiff Right Hand has been testament to that for the last few years and gained over 40,000 followers. I love debate. I encourage it. We live in a time where it's needed now more than ever and yet here we are seeing people cancelled or shunned for their own personal views. It's obscene, and it's deeply wrong.

My view is if someone comes up to me and wants to discuss how much 'research' they've done, I'll automatically ask which books they've been reading. Because at least the library has the fucking decency to separate the fiction section.

Talking of politics, I fear that Boris Johnson will not be the man to be remembered fondly like Churchill but instead a man who relied on Churchillian rhetoric to bumble through a time when the country needed a solid leader. Anyway, no more Political shit.

We have seen the rise in the cult of fake news thanks to old President Trump. A legitimate questioning of the unscrupulous media but done by an equally unscrupulous 'politician'. He single handedly used the cult of personality to maximum effect and gave credence to the Q Anon brigade. A highly triggered cult of their own who alarmingly think that 'evidence' of such things as Princess Diana's faked death and satanic paedophilic groups and secret tunnels is widely available on, wait for it......YouTube.

When questioned they either meet you with self-satisfied grins on their faces, as if they are party to some special information the rest of us don't know about, or get hostile very fucking quickly. It's opium for red necks.

I have to say as soon as I hear people talking about 'They' I immediately switch off. That's when you know the conversation is beyond repair. 'They'. So invested are these folk in the Illuminati and the Rothschilds that 'They' is now good enough to encompass everything.

Having said that, it makes life a little bit more interesting thinking that everything has all been planned. The thought that things sometimes just happen is never up for debate as it tears a hole in the entire thing. Chaos is frightening. Conspiracy is comforting. But I'm not one for the cancel culture of censorship, far from it, so let's all discuss it. I'm pro debate. Mass debate you might say....

My podcast Stiff Right Hand has been testament to that for the last few years and gained over 40,000 followers. I love debate. I encourage it. We live in a time where it's needed now more than ever and yet here we are seeing people cancelled or shunned for their own personal views. It's obscene, and it's deeply wrong.

My view is if someone comes up to me and wants to discuss how much 'research' they've done, I'll automatically ask which books they've been reading. Because at least the library has the fucking decency to separate the fiction section.

Talking of politics, I fear that Boris Johnson will not be the man to be remembered fondly like Churchill but instead a man who relied on Churchillian rhetoric to bumble through a time when the country needed a solid leader. Anyway, no more Political shit, if you wanted that you'd have bought Private Eye from the newsagent presumably wouldn't you?

Back then March 2020 I sat down for four months and emptied my soul into my previous book, and I can't tell you how thrilled I was with the response from everyone. The first week alone the sales were extraordinary, and people were rifling through it in days, some in just a couple of days. It took me four fucking months, seven hours a day to write that and people were consuming it like a shot of whisky. I didn't know whether I should be flattered or disappointed. I guess the fact that it was so easy to read is a compliment. There's nothing worse than a book that's like chewing an old bit of gristle.

But the general consensus was that it was a journey that people were compelled to read even if they weren't fans of wrestling per se. I was happy with that, it's always what I hoped my wrestling events would be, something that could be enjoyed by everyone not just the basement dwelling nerds who silently critique everything with sneering disregard.

Not that I have anything against wrestling fans or those who cater specifically to them It's just always been important to me that anything I do in wrestling appeals to as many people as possible, and to never put all my eggs in one basket. It's always worked out best for me that way. Plus, like it or not, families spend more money than the internet virgins.

During Lockdown I saw the business I love crumble away and wash into the sea, leaving wrestlers clinging on by their fingertips holding on for dear life. That is in no way a melodramatic analogy either in case you think I'm taking the piss. People who were once self-assured performers were splitting up from their partners and going into meltdowns. Veterans literally sobbing and banging their heads against the tombstone of wrestling like Greyfriars Bobby, doing anything they could do keep the fires burning. Obviously nothing compared to the poor buggers who'd been affected by covid and lost loved ones, but seeing people suddenly having the carpet of life ripped out from under them was still a horrible thing.

Some were making videos online to try and gain followers on social media platforms by doing berserk stunts. It just reeked of desperation, it was akin to a child in a room full of adults doing shit magic tricks in the corner trying to get attention. Like a massive tear stained army of screaming man children who weren't hugged enough as toddlers. It was embarrassing. Truly embarrassing."Look at me mumma, I done wiped my own ass!!"

I wrote my fucking book much to people's astonishment. "Ooh did you have a ghost writer??" They'd ask. No prick, guess what, I managed it on my own. Imagine that, not cutting corners and getting shit done.

My wife started Maid of Muscle. These silly cunts in British wrestling were wearing tea towels on their heads or jumping into a bath of cold baked beans to get attention. Social media became awash with the wrestling public turning into children and slapping their own heads like Dustin Hoffman in Rain Man because there were no shows. These people must've been milk monitors at school. Shock and horror dear reader!

Imagine Sir Ian McKellen doing that "I'm sorry there's no theatres open at the moment, so here's me dancing the Macarena with a mop". Fuck off! 2020 was without a shadow of a doubt the Chinese year of the Cunt.

People lost loved ones. Many lost their dignity. I had friends of mine who had served in the forces and dodged bullets for their country calling me up in tears because their

businesses were crashing down around them. I was sat in the very room I'm writing this in now, trying with everything I could muster to talk down people from doing something daft. Ironic considering I am very much the King of Daft, but I knew that we would get through this. Bad times don't last. You can't repair a lost life, but everything else can be rebuilt, that's what us Brits can do. Its inbuilt in us.

So, as I have racked my brains on how to start this difficult second book Christmas has just been and gone - as has 2020 thankfully. However, the wife and I didn't manage to dodge the inevitable grasp of Covid.

We'd all had a torrid year, and I fully expected it to be a beautiful Christmas because of it. People forced to reject consumerism and enjoy being at home with their loved ones. It couldn't go wrong surely as the whole sodding year by that token had prepared us for Christmas day.

Yes, as I start our journey ending the biblical shit house of a year that was 2020, Tarn's dry cough and my thumping headache developed out of hand on Boxing Day. After a beautiful Christmas day with my mum Peggy, and having spoiled our beloved dogs Milo and Luna with a lunatic array of squeaky things to kill, we got to the point the following day where we attended a drive-thru Covid station. I insisted upon it. It really felt like you had someone else's head on and were walking through treacle. But the lure of a drive-thru test centre was too exciting for me. Perhaps shiny robots would put things up my bum, I just had to see it. What a time to be alive ladies and gentlemen. "Have you ever been fisted by a robot??" Ooh Matron.

Who'd have thought it eh, it was like something out of a movie, although clearly not the one I had in mind. A slickly prepared wasteland with tunnels and slip-roads punctuated with Portacabins and, as it was Boxing Day after all, an astonishing amount of staff on hand. All remarkably cheerful, helpful, young and good looking. All taking turns to shout different instructions at me like I was a mad old bastard. When I went to put the window down they'd shoot backwards as if I'd drawn a hand gun. I thought "Well really, this is bat shit".

So, we pull into our bay. Now I must say it's been many a year since I'd pulled up in my car and made a woman gag, but that's precisely what I did here as we took turns putting these swabs down the back of our throat, and sat like nitwits dry heaving until tears rolled down our cheeks, then up the old bugle for good measure. Boxing Day used to be about watching Bond, playing Call of Duty and eating cold cuts and pickles, but here we were, wrapped up jabbing sticks into our faces next to a car with an elderly couple sat in it who I'm pretty fucking sure were having a picnic. Chequered blanket, flask, the lot, having a fucking grand old day out at the Covid drive-thru. That's Bexhill on Sea for you in a nutshell.

So where were we last time? Ah yes, my wrestling promotion Extreme World Wrestling was in its third incarnation after our raw early days where we were the young, sneering, arrogant goth kids putting our middle fingers up to the old school and introducing the British wrestling scene to our own brand of punk, loud music, dancing girls, live pythons, blood and everything else we could throw at it. We were a right little bunch of edge lords, but at the time it fucking worked and if you weren't with us - you were against us. We were emblazoned all over the glossy wrestling magazines month after month, and the so called 'wrestling purists' fucking hated us.

EWW wasn't what you'd call polished by today's standards in terms of, well, anything really, but it captured the attention of fans up and down the country who wanted to see what the next show would conjure up. We were the first promotion to use pyrotechnics in the UK, and even that was flying by the seat of our pants and on more than one occasion almost involved some of our young assistants getting blown sky high!

15

Those fans from the late nineties stayed loyal to us to this day. Wherever I've travelled, they've followed. I'm not the messiah, I'm a very naughty boy.

That's the most remarkable thing of all when I stop to look back at it. Most wrestling shows throughout the land just present wrestling. It's not a show, it's a self-congratulatory exhibition of the art of wrestling. Therefore, you will only draw limited fans to it as it's a very niche subculture, it always has been.

I was extremely wise looking back on it as a lad in my early 20's to figure out what was needed, and in doing so aligned myself with Jamie Clubb from the world famous Chipperfield Circus family. It was more than chance, it was fate, and having always been a fan of variety shows, the classic three ring circus where everything is going off in different directions, I realised that we would hook more than just families, yes, we'd upset the clipboard internet brigade who'd sit on their hands and spend as little money as possible and just turn up to whisper to their mates how they'd have done it better, but we would attract fans of music, theatre, cinema and storytelling of all kinds. Fans of the macabre and fans of fantasy who wanted to see the bad guys vanquished. Guess fucking what? We succeeded.

It was the best four years I could've hoped for, it was intoxicating at times receiving phone calls from the elder statesmen of wrestling who would try and unsettle us or hope to stop our run, and oh boy did we have a run.

I remember some even went as far as threatening to show up and try and turn us over. Nobody ever turned up. Pretending to be a hard man in pro wrestling is like pretending to be a hard man in Premier League football; everyone knows you're all fart and no poo. So jog that nonsense on.

I still get messages to this very day from people who watched us from afar as fledgling wrestlers, who wanted to be a part of what was then Extreme World Warfare back in 1999, but were too afraid to contact us or approach us at shows because they'd heard on the grapevine that we were an occult cult. Something that Jamie and I took great pleasure in.

So my point dear reader, is that although the first run was short it laid such a solid foundation, and captured people's attention to such a formidable degree, that they stayed entranced by our every move, even to this very day. The most loyal fans of all are right here in EWW.

Tarn and I were wrestling around Europe quite often in Belgium, Holland, Germany and France and, as much as I always hated the rigmarole of travelling, it was fun doing
it with her there with me. It was a breeze as a youngster flying around but, as with everything, it gets more tiresome with age. Unlike the days of doing shows in Europe before where I'd just arrive and get to the venue, this time around I'd insist on a day longer so we could at least have time to do a little sightseeing while we were there too. I was more than happy to take bookings if it would mean Tarn was getting experience, I had turned down easily a couple of dozen European gigs from 2010 to 2015 if the Promoter just wanted me. I had no interest in furthering my career, the whole point of the job for me now was to make sure Tarn had opportunities, and as someone who didn't even have a passport when we met, I wanted her to see a bit of the world.
If she wasn't part of the package then I didn't do business, as I never needed any booking that badly. If she wasn't needed, I'd never take a European gig at all, and only a handful of British gigs, where I'd end up many a time sat like a miserable prick in a locker room full of idiots I didn't know, who were prancing and preening and pretending they were superstars, whilst thinking to myself "What the fuck am I doing here?".
The bell would ring and I'd go out there and punk out some little twerp in half the time the promoter actually wanted, taken my money and gone home. Yes, it's arsehole behaviour, and I don't recommend anyone ever treat the business with that much contempt, but as time in the business was passing by so was my patience with idiots.

I read an online review of a show I did for a guy call Dan Read. The fan wrote, 'It didn't appear that Dominator really wanted to be here'. Why, don't you have a keen eye young man?

The older I got, the less I wanted to go on last. And as someone who often had shorter, smash mouth appearances rather than competitive matches, I was always happy to come into a promotion as an 'attraction' rather than a regular roster member. Less pressure really plus I don't need a belt, nor did I particularly need a big fan base, but I have always liked being a person who nobody knows what they're going to get when I walk through the curtain. Will he really have the hump and put someone in hospital? Will he pull someone out of the crowd? Will he break character and have a dance?

The daft thing is I often didn't know what I was going to do half the time, and I mean that. I've got bored halfway through a match and literally said, "Fuck it" and finished it. Again, not something I'm proud of, but I'm just being honest. I've probably upset people who have paid good money for me or had faith in me, and they've been too scared or polite to say anything, and at times I've thrown that back at them.

When you're wrestling you've got to 'switch up' when the red light comes on or when the curtain is pulled back. If you're not engaged by that thought then it's time to jack it in, or certainly re-evaluate where you stand in the business.

Eventually I realised that if I wasn't travelling with close friends or my wife, then I probably shouldn't be taking bookings anywhere for any price because I no longer enjoyed the driving, and certainly no longer wanted to be backstage with these people. If you weren't talking about wrestling, they were stuck for conversation. Sport, Politics, World affairs, forget it. These new kids were without a doubt the most uninteresting, blinkered and dare I say 'thick' group I'd ever come across. It was like a Napoleon Dynamite convention.

I spoke to a chap once who worked quite high up for the BBC, when we did Distraction for Jimmy Carr in 2005, and he had said to me "People don't want to be in awe of celebrity anymore, they want to be able to relate to them".

That immediately stuck in my head and related straight away to what has to be the mindset of many young wrestlers getting into the job; not wanting to be larger than life like those who came before, because practising backflips on trampolines at your mum's house is far easier than the dedication it takes to build your physique up to look like the credible fighter you're meant to be portraying.

Imagine having the aura to hold an audience in the palm of your hand by just walking through a curtain. Now these silly little trick midgets are doing tumbling acts and have all the presence of a fucking Lasagne, rushing through 'sequences' without letting anything register, and each stunt has to be more ludicrous than the last and just as contrived, ad nauseum, until eventually what have you got left?

Now the main difference I see are a group of individuals who've never had a real fight in their life, trying to portray combat and occasionally tripping over themselves trying

their hardest to make it look as phoney as humanly possible. All very peculiar. Throw in much shorter careers, and bugger all to fall back on into the bargain, and that just about sums it up unless you're one of the top earners. And even then, if your face doesn't fit and you're kicked out of the nest like the slew of WWE NXT hopefuls who are binned off, make sure you get yourself a trade or if you haven't already, an education. Otherwise, you'll end up delivering pizza and wondering what the fuck just happened. No fucker ever told me that, and if they had I probably wouldn't have listened. So, here's me wasting my time by telling you.

At this point for me I was now just bashing people or getting high and not performing, when actually saying 'No' to the booking in the first place would've been the sensible option. I was getting unprofessional because I hated being around it but, like a fly to shit being the best analogy here, I was finding it hard to avoid.

I was no longer in love with wrestling, how could I be if being asked to do a show was making me see red. Can you believe that? I resented being asked to perform.

I'd actually built this up in my head to such an irrational degree that I'd get angry about having to perform for people. Mental really, but I've no excuse. I can put my finger on when this mentality started. I wrestled a lot between 2008 and 2013, and was taking on more shows than I really needed to, and as the years went by the old faces started to disappear and the locker rooms of old that were full of buzz and dare I say 'banter', were now replaced with a new breed of wrestler who was coming through. There was less camaraderie and more a group of lads who wanted to have the best match of the night, fuck anyone else. They were the school milk monitors; the kids who were play acting as hard men. Surprisingly they took themselves incredibly seriously too.

If you've made a name for yourself in this job then that's great, you can't knock success in any form, but if you're on your way up or on the bottom rung, don't act like you're hot shit.

I did a show for LDN somewhere in Essex, and after my match realised that I hadn't any wipes to get rid of the face paint around my eyes. I asked a young lad, Alan Travis, if he could grab me some tissue or rag that I could use. He tapped his Championship belt that he'd been wearing all day, looked me in the eyes with all the innocence of a child and said in a quivering voice, "But I'm the Champion". I said "And I won't ask you twice" and he scurried off to fetch me a kitchen roll. Every day's a school day.

I noticed that there were no actual hard men who looked like they wanted to just go out there and break your neck. People you feared. People like me. Even the All-Star crew looked like men and that they could at the very least have a fight. Wasn't that the point of all this??

There was a cookie cutter type of wrestler on shows the length and breadth of the country, Promoted by young men like Sanjay Bagga, a guy who to his credit had promoted very regularly, but was now fixated on a certain look - young lads with abs and a vacant grin. These characteristics I couldn't relate to.

I could see the way wrestling was going. Less big men, less colourful character, and a bizarre need to try and convince the audience that they were watching something legitimate all whilst doing bizarre and highly choreographed 'sequences' that were more contrived than anything I'd ever seen.

They were trying to make the product more believable whilst at the same time presenting Cirque du Soleil with the stars of Grange Hill.

I always gave them something more than legitimate to watch. When you're dressed in latex spikes with face painted, and have a name that sounds like a widows delight on sale at Ann Summers, it pays to put your money where your mouth is. But apparently the done thing was to ditch the fancy gimmick names and colourful outfits, and all wear black and do 'Strictly Come Dancing' style Lindy hop sequences to get a reaction for the boys in the back.

I'd sit backstage at these shows, LDN, Wrestleforce, HEW and the various promotions in Europe, and watch as the grapplers on the rosters got smaller and smaller in stature, like Russian dolls, with not an intimidating character amongst them. It was like groups of young supply teachers with Lego haircuts who were all moonlighting at the weekend.

My dad took me to watch the wrestling when I was a kid. From the British to the American scene, I was in awe of them because they looked bulletproof, like superheroes. Not only that, but the action also looked authentic, like a competition, a struggle. Not one of them looked like I could take them clean out with an open hand slap either, not like this group of pretenders.

I'm pretty sure that was when I emotionally checked out. Yep, that was it.

CHAPTER TWO
KING WEZ

It was around 2013 now. We were living on Hastings seafront opposite the burnt out Pier, with our beautiful English Bull Terrier Evo. He loved it there, as it was a Victorian flat with buttresses and decorative fleur de lys and, more importantly, huge corridors that were ideal for him to perform his party piece 'The Hucklebutt'.

All Bull Terriers have the same ludicrous characteristics, this was one of them, which as my grandmother would've described as 'a funny five minutes' . He'd go totally statue still, tail pointed out at the back and a glazed expression would come over him. Then he'd haul ass at top speed and, with remarkable navigation, do figure of eights around the living room, zooming in and out of chairs and tables like fucking lightening. It was hilarious and he'd go like the clappers.

I'll never forget my old mate and best man at our wedding, Jerry, at a Barbecue at my parents on their huge back lawn in Oxfordshire when, seeing this for the first time, told anyone who'd listen that Evo was "The incredible mathematical genius, Mr Eves" as Jerry would shout out maths to him "Six plus two" or "12 minus 4" and Evo would scamper around in a figure of eight with Jerry loudly proclaiming him to be a "Canine prodigy".

Ginny and Jerry I wrote about briefly in Simply the Beast. Two very important people in my life. Ginny and I worked with for many years at The Blue Cross Animal rescue. I fell in in love with her on my first week there, she was tall with piercing eyes and this long-tousled hair, she reminded me of Glenn Close in Fatal Attraction. I told her that too.

It was the really hot summer of 1995 and, knowing I was the new boy on the firm, she asked if I'd like to join her for lunch. Me being completely and utterly useless at socialising with normal people after surrendering to my early wrestling career, totally forgot about this and drove into town on my own, only to return to my desk to find a little cauldron and a toy bunny in it that she'd cobbled together in typical genius invention from the merchandise stand in Reception. This hilarious concoction was accompanied by a handwritten note saying 'Forget someone did we?? Yours sincerely....Glenn'

Well, I'll be fucked if that wasn't an absolute master stroke. I realised then what a cracker Gin was, and we became firm friends from that day on.

There was one day where I pushed it a bit far though. It was a freezing December Friday afternoon, and it had snowed heavily across the Cotswold fields that our offices backed onto. During a harmless snowball fight with her colleagues, I got carried away and spear tackled Gin out of her wellies. That went down like a fart in church.

Anyhow, she went on to marry this long legged loony called Jerry, whom I was superbly pranked into meeting at a lovely pub one afternoon. I used to go to lunch with Ginny most days, after being too afraid to forget following the bunny boiling incident, and one day this grey-haired old bastard turned up on a motorbike, removed his helmet, swept his long grey hair back and before our basket of chips had arrived had Gin swooning at the bar like some silly schoolgirl. She'd got up mid conversation with me and said "Cor, who's he?"

I can tell you dear reader, I was fucking livid. Of course, they'd played me like a fiddle. I said to my mate, also called Stuart who was sitting next to me "Who's that cunt?"

Anyway, the whole thing was designed to make me look the cunt as they were all in on it. An elaborate introduction, but one that was totally fitting for a man who I shall never ever forget. He became a firm friend, and I can honestly say is one of the funniest people I've ever met in my life.

Of course, Jerry never fucking let me forget our first meeting, and even threw that story in for good measure in his Best Man's speech at our wedding, although embellished it beautifully to the point where we'd gone on to fight for hours in the hot sun!

He was quite a character was old Jerry, a long-distance lorry driver who had driven all across Europe and had some incredible stories of his own. A former addict in his youth he now had Hepatitis which had led to a series of nasty biopsies, but he'd meet everything head on with incredible humour and laid back reasoning, I admired him hugely, he owned his illness.

On my downtime from work and wrestling I'd spend many happy hours with Ginny and Jerry, they were like my adoptive hippy mentors. I'd bring over a giant carrier bag with enormous hunks of home-grown from my dear old pal Pistol Pete, who was a giant nutcase of a man who walked around with a Bowler Hat on shouting at people. He did tremendous deals in this particular range I have to say. Salt of the earth to Jerry he was, mad old Pete.

We'd sit for hours smoking and laughing into the early hours. I remember taking a whole week out during the World Cup in Japan in 2002, (yes, we'd kept this merry act up for many years) We'd be smoking ourselves stupid during an England game, I'd send my cronies to get us McDonald's, and then we'd sit talking absolute bollocks. Watching William Shatner doing forward rolls on car bonnets and stuffing cars in to hedges on TJ Hooker as Jerry would shout "Yes, very sound Policing that is!" at the television.

Jerry loved a bit of chaos in the news, he'd have been fascinated by Donald Trump and Covid. I remember when the United States bombarded Fallujah and Ginny would say "Jerry's at home, he's been watching the Fallujah show all day".

They moved to this incredible little thatched cottage which I mentioned before, like the Weasley house in Harry Potter, every corner had something to catch the eye. A furry bat on a beam or a screaming gargoyle high on the brick work, smell of Nag Champa and you'd sink into it upon entry, it was like climbing into a hot bath, just heaven really. The best bit for me was that old King Jerry hated having to leave it as he was happy laughing at the madness unfolding in the world on his television set, he was like an old gargoyle, part of the fixtures. Even when Tarn and I would drive down to Warwickshire to visit them he wouldn't leave his chair as I'd gurn through the window at him upon arrival, a long bony finger would point at me and these mischievous hooded eyes would peer through the smoke at me like a lunatic Octopus on Marijuana. He was like a tall, rangy Clint Eastwood but with soft eyes. I can't tell you the fucking nonsense we used to get up to, I often think about it during those times when you're struggling to get to sleep, that's when it'll hit me, and I'll find myself laughing out loud.

It was at this time in 2013 that Ginny and Jerry came to visit us in Hastings. I have so many Jerry stories, but I'm going to tell this one as it always stands out in my head.

Jerry was always fascinated by Hastings. He used to park up at the Stade lorry park, decades before we'd met, to have a sleep after coming back from Dover. He said Hastings was the place where old junkies came to die. He had a soft spot for Rye, and loved the Mermaid inn which sat high atop an old cobbled street. He found Hastings comical though and that always tickled me.

The first time he and Gin came to visit me in Hastings when I first moved down here in 2007 we were walking past the amusements. Jerry insisted we go on the Ghost Train. The surly old boy running it came shambling over with a cigarette stuck to his bottom lip and ushered us all into the same carriage, and a lad gave us a push as we rattled through this fucking dark tunnel, it was so spectacularly shit. I think Jerry got hit on the head with a baked bean can on a bit of string. We were fucking howling with laughter as it was just rubbish in there. There was a sheet stuck to the wall and Jerry feigned horror, throwing his spindly arms in the air, turning to me saying "Did you see, that cunt nearly had me you know". Our asses were stuck to the seats literally to top it off, it was a mucky, low rent affair. Just what we'd wanted.

We then walked past the swans; giant boats shaped like swans on a little boating lake. The mystique of which was totally blown as we walked past to see a young lad walking in the middle of the 'lake', water not even up to his shins, fishing a dead seagull out of the water. Jerry threw his head back and laughed at the abject misery of the whole scene.

We would sit at home and smoke ourselves into oblivion while the girls went off into Eastbourne on the train for the day. We'd watch films and talk utter bollocks. We honestly had no idea how much we'd consumed and were pretty fucked it must be said. Jerry was a big fan of this legal high called Spice, which as I understand it from some of my pals is a potent currency in prison.

It wasn't long after the girls returned that Jerry turned to me and asked about the train service.

26

"Who's the man in charge of Southern rail these days?" He said earnestly.

What a peculiar thing to ask I thought. But not as fucking mental as what was yet to come.

"It's Bernard Cribbins isn't it?" He said with a straight face.

I looked at Ginny in horror and she collapsed on the sofa absolutely howling with laughter.

I said "What, the bloke off the Railway children??"

He stopped and looked down for a minute and said "Oh god I'm fucked Gin"

We'd consumed so much Spice we didn't know what was going on, and he'd peeled off before me in spectacular fashion and was sitting in silence, but every ten minutes would suddenly come out with some phenomenal bollocks with such belief that you'd question your own sanity.

"What year was it you got involved with the Hotel Industry?" he said to me

I sat puzzled again as Ginny interjected "Jerry that was your father".

To which he'd mumble "Oh fuck" and sink back into the chair looking defeated again.

Tarn was making dinner for us in the adjoining kitchen as Jerry kept shouting out, "Go on do that dance again, you know that one you did earlier." We were all looking at each other, completely gobsmacked as to what he was going to say next, he was convinced he was in another universe.

I had put a film on, 'Hobo with a Shotgun', and he kept saying "When's this going to start for fucks sake, Gin", all annoyed, "This adverts been going on for ages."

The film had already been on for an hour at least.

We had a huge futon mattress laid out on the living room floor for them to sleep on. Jerry would all of a sudden get a burst of energy and leap at Tarn for a wrestle and say "Come on, let's be havin ya".

In a heartbeat he was spun upside down and thrown across the room landing on the mattress saying "Fuck me Gin she ain't half strong. Come on, best of three!!"

Before conceding defeat.

We'd had over a decade of nonsense together Ginny, Jerry and I, and their company and humour had seen me through some really difficult times in my life, knowing they were there was always a huge source of comfort to me. He wasn't allowed to drink alcohol of any kind due to the damage done to his liver by the Hep C, but he was remarkably disciplined on that front I have to say. However now and again he was allowed a bit of a smoke up.

Jerry said that weekend "Fuck me mate, this is probably the last time we'll be able to have a blow out like this together." I didn't think anything of that statement. It was just another bit of Jerry's home spun wisdom. But he was right.

Tarn took the phone-call from Ginny on the 10th of May 2013. Jerry had died of a brain haemorrhage.

Ginny along with a handful of friends who were able to get there in time were at his bedside.

I can't tell you, my heart sank hearing that, like a stone. Tarn and I held each other and sobbed for ages. I've never quite felt as much like a permanent light had gone out as much as that moment. It's indescribable really. I was so grateful that Tarn had got to know him and was able to understand my grief. Something so completely different to that of my father's death, and I don't know why. But by god did it hurt. As much as I think of things he'd say or daft things we did that catch me unawares, there's times when I want to call him to tell him something that has happened and which I know would've amused him. Not only that, I've never seen a couple in all my life as complete and harmonious as Ginny and Jerry and my heart was torn for her. Even their arguments I'd refer to as 'Trouble in Toy Town' as they'd just be rubbish compared to anyone else's real rows. Jerry would always laugh at that.

She'd made a wonderful life with Jerry, and he knew he'd done well for himself and loved Ginny more than anything. Equally, he knew he wasn't long for the world but owned it all the same, which is the mark of the man in my book.

We'd often discuss his mortality in front of his roaring fire when Gin would go up to bed and he'd sit forward in his chair and peer at me and say "Fuck me I've done alright haven't I Baby Stuey?" He'd call me that after the Family Guy character, which amused him no end.

Jerry's funeral was on the 23rd May at The Church of St Peter and St Paul in the beautiful village of Butlers Marston where they lived.

Now the most beautiful part of this traumatic time happened the night before the funeral. Tarn and I drove down, and Jerry had been brought home and was laid out beautifully in a natural wicker casket. For the first time ever, as we turned the corner into the beautiful Butlers Marston where Bryher Cottage would suddenly appear and you knew everything was alright, it felt different. This was always our safe place, our happy commune away from violence and the shit the world kicks up, you know?

I parked up and there was Ginny to greet us. Eyes full and we all three hugged tightly for ages.

She was so relieved to see us it was an incredible outpouring of love and grief; one I've never seen before or since I have to say. She was so keen for us to come inside and see him. He always had his chair, which he'd be Lord and Baron from, right by the wood burner. The casket was on trestles right in front of that, and he looked just terrific. I cannot begin to do justice to this by writing alone, but we had sat in that very room, actually fucking talking about this moment, for years. It always felt like a daft anecdote that would just be like a carousel we'd ride forever, but here we were. Surreal doesn't cover it.

I have to say, the Undertakers from Warwickshire had done a splendid job with the old King.

As someone who has laid out hundreds of deceased to be viewed by their families, and at this point had been in the funeral business for six years, I knew that the best thing you can always ever hope for is that you will be able to provide, at the very least, a peaceful and pleasant lasting memory of that person. It's the greatest thing you can do for somebody in my opinion, and a real privilege.

By that token, they'd done the old boy proud, they'd taken years off him, and he looked quite literally serene and, dare I say, beautiful. That was one of his daft trademark sayings, "Am I not beautiful?".

So there you go Jerry, you've got it in writing now - yes, you are.

We sat there that night, our last night together, with Ginny in Jerry's. He was at such an angle that the joss stick Gin had lit made it look like he was enjoying one last blaze for the road. She said, "It doesn't seem right without him butting in does it?"

It didn't. But it felt incredibly right all the same.

The morning of the funeral, Ginny and her sisters and friends gathered around weaving flowers into the wicker coffin from their own stunning garden. Now most blokes I know would dream of a Viking funeral with flames and arrows peppering the sky. All Jerry would've ever wanted would've been a group of beautiful, tearful women fussing around him and telling tales of how wonderful he was, and he got just that. I just stood back and watched. It was simply perfect actually.

In fact I can say this, as I remember him saying to Tarn, "Course I want you at my funeral in a fascinator and veil, all gorgeous birds sobbing". Like all Kings, he got his wish.

I carried Jerry into church, not on my own of course. I won't go too much into the funeral other than two details I want to share. I see thousands of eulogies every year. I admire anyone who can do that for their partner or parent. But just like Tarnya's eulogy for her mother which was a powerhouse performance, Ginny's was quite remarkable, and she absolutely glowed. I can't tell you. She spoke so well with the huge gathering in the church hanging on every word, it was a stunning eulogy in her own gentle and loving way. She's the most kindhearted girl I've ever met is Ginny, and I feared for her that day if I'm totally honest, and I shouldn't have. She was immense.

30

Seeing my dear friends Jamie Clubb and my old housemate Tom Conroy there was great. Both had spent time with Jerry and they were very fond of him.

Finally at the crematorium I inevitably crumpled when I heard the opening salvo of bass drum to start 'Live Forever' by Oasis. Tarn had previously told Ginny that's what Jerry always spoke about for his funeral, and so there it was. Christ, I cried my eyes out. I still struggle to listen to that song to this day. I'm funny about emotion, some people have a natural ability to use it very positively. Maybe it's not natural, maybe they're just good at tapping into their reserves, I don't know. It crushes me inside though and makes it a frightening place. I wish it didn't.

Ginny often used to be the first of the group at Bryher to peel off and go to bed in the wee hours of our nights together. She would tell me that it gave her immense comfort to hear Jerry and I utterly helpless with laughter downstairs. There were times I truly thought the cause of death on my death certificate would read 'Laughter', he had me in fucking pieces.

I'll never forget you old King Wez you mad bastard. The world's a much darker place without you in it, but I know I'll see you again one day.

CHAPTER THREE
WICKY WICKY WILD WILD WEST

Things were changing again, and we moved into two new venues. My Extreme Academy of Wrestling had now outgrown The Hive which was owned by a good friend Carl Denne, owner of HKA kickboxing. It was literally the perfect set up to start things off, as I spoke about in my first book, as it had a real dungeon atmosphere there, much like Stu Harts infamous Dungeon in Calgary and of course Skullkrushers where I had trained.

But now we were attracting larger numbers, because increasing numbers at our shows and word of mouth was bringing a lot of young people to our school.

I was the sole teacher at this point, and we had Tarn who was still closely under my tutelage, Dave, Matty, Len, Jordan, Alfie, Deano, Jonk, Rue, along with one of my first ever students Greg and of course young Taylor, who came to our early Hastings and Herne Bay shows as a young boy and was now a very promising part of the academy.

We were now in the position to move on from The Hive and went into the building where we've been ever since, Fighting Tigers, now known as Raw Performance.

A huge facility that housed many fantastic schools, Olly Thompson of UFC fame trained there along with the awesome Tolly Plested who taught there, this was as well as a host of other great local fighters and Kickboxing champions. British boxing legend Robbie Read was on hand too and stopped by to watch our kids from the Academy on one occasion.

With a huge expanse of floor for sparring, a solid ring and caged area upstairs it was a fighter's dream, and me and my band of idiots have been there ever since.

At this point our shows were pulling in big numbers and we were having to turn people away at the door which is both enviable and unenviable. It came at the perfect time when the premises was up for sale and forced our hand to move into our second move, into the much bigger venue Kings Church, which was a remarkable building in Hastings.

I spoke about this a little at the end of the last book. It was a modern Baptist building with a light rig that the 02 would've been proud of. I'd tried to get us into this venue a couple of years previously, but the previous minister turned his nose up at the thought of professional wrestling, but the new minister, a young and very dynamic young man called Santino, championed us, being that he was a fan of pro wrestling growing up in New York - and so the rest was history.

What a great team they were, a full tech team on hand and state of the art facilities, even a merchandise foyer, it was a promoter's dream come true. Not cheap, but I knew if we worked hard we could fill this huge venue with little trouble and really make it count. Being Baptist they were all extremely upbeat high on life, they would be busying themselves around this huge centre on giant cherry pickers, adjusting the lights and putting all the tech details in order way before the ring would turn up. Such is wrestling life.

Some of our greatest matches and events were held there over the next few years, and I shall tell you about all of them, including probably my greatest match of all which I still love to this day. The real deal sealer for me was the giant video wall, which was literally a huge cinema screen that yawned over the top of the entrance ramp-way. This got my creative juices flowing straight away.

From our early days at the Olympiad, Jamie and I wanted to be the first to create backstage promos or cut away videos between matches to play to the audience. We now had the perfect set-up, with a sound system to boot. We had a big show coming up called Survival of the Sickest, which pitted both sides of the company against each other. The good guys, a band of young renegades led by the daredevil leader Skarlett who was technically still finding her style and was by no means the finished article. I wanted her to have more flair in her performance and be less reckless, she still had these spindly 'Bambi on ice' legs, and it doesn't matter how fundamentally strong your core is, if you've not found your 'ring legs' you ain't ready my friend. She did however at that stage have a great following, and obviously the Skarlett character had the guts and look to be the Team captain. Visually it was so right.

They would take on Death Row, led by me, who was now a hated villain after turning my back on my own wife in violent style. I was joined by my tag partner Charlie Rage, the now legendary Jynx, Exodus and Philip Bateman. This was to be the headlining match of Survival of the Sickest and we were pushing this heavily at the time, even selling Limited Edition T shirts with just me and Skarlett on the front. Team Extreme Vs Death Row - choose your side. They sold out in days; we knew it was going to be a big one.

During one of our writing meetings, Tarn, myself and Liam Dowe put our heads together for how we were going to promote this and make it our biggest one yet as it was the culmination of a couple of years' worth of storytelling.

In 2012 I accompanied Tarn on a photo shoot for a well-known fantasy photographer called Victor Kurzweil who was holding a giant themed shoot with models from all over Europe at a place called Laredo in Kent, a remarkable Wild West Town that's been used for movies, commercials etc. Tarn had done her fair share of modelling for Goth and Metal publications and although this was a very different scenario, what a fun day it was. I was still reeling from a nasty bout of pneumonia and of course typically it pissed down that day, but it all added to the authenticity of the shoot with a mud spattered town and gloom.

Victor got some incredible shots of Tarn and I, armed to the teeth walking down the centre of the mud tracked road between the Saloon bars, Undertakers and snake oil sellers. Tarn was the Sheriff and I was her 'heavy'. Well what else could I fucking be, right?

The other actors and models there all stood under cover of the awnings watching us stride through the mud. We were soaked, but the results were outstanding.

So, the point of this story. We've got two teams, a main event shrouded in a strong storyline, and a giant cinema video wall to open the show up to the people with a powerful cinematic masterpiece. It was a no-brainer - let's make a mini movie at Laredo.

Liam and I made a road trip to meet with the people there. It was right out in the sticks, it was already like a movie set a few miles before arriving, 'The Hills Have Eyes' sprang to mind. I had to pull over for a shit at this old garage. Heaps of old cars dumped high like a wrecking yard on top of each other. Eventually this old boy came out and showed me where the toilet was. Having been to Laredo I didn't think there would be much chance of finding one there.

Now I like a good toilet anecdote. Tarn gets angry with me when we wrestle abroad because I must explore toilets at every pub, bar, restaurant or place we visited. I've been in toilets all over the world you know. I'm not a secret cottager or anything sordid, I just enjoy seeing them.

But this was something else, it was all tiled and moss was on the windowsills, but the best bit was an unbroken giant sheet of cobweb that I walked through much like Indiana Jones and the Temple of Doom (the bog years).

So, like all blokes needing a turn out, I hastily dropped my trousers and pinched one out, my arse not quite touching the frozen seat. Then hey presto, you guessed it, no fucking toilet paper. Not a shit ticket in sight. I've heard of people doing what I did next, and this was my first time of doing it, but I removed one sock and wiped my ass with it. And no, I didn't put it back on again. I went around Laredo that day with an itchy arse and one sock missing. You've got to paint the picture haven't you ladies and gentlemen.

Back to our mini-masterpiece, we filmed some short cut aways from different angles, met the man in charge, made the payment and pencilled in the date for a few hours of filming there the following month. Liam was blown away with the place, it must be seen to be believed. We walked through a big old horse field and then this stunning old town just looms up on the horizon, it really is a bit special. We set about drawing up a story board for it that very afternoon. It was to be a mix of people involved in the Main event and a scattering of my students on the undercard who would make cameos.

The day arrived for filming and we went up in a convoy of several vehicles. There was me, Tarn, Jonk, Phil and his wife at the time Helen, Johnny, Dave, Greg, Matty, Rue and of course Liam.

We all got changed above the Saloon bar which all had individual bedrooms all done out exactly as you'd expect with sepia pictures on the tables and walls, and a certain musty smell. Like stepping back in time, no detail was spared.

With Skarlett as the Sheriff and the local reprobates, Dave, Greg and Liam playing cards, Jonk was at the Ironmongers pounding away at some Horseshoes, overseen by Helen looking on with her top hat on standing outside the Funeral Parlour.

The opening scene shows the length of the street taken from high as a lantern blows in the wind and a rocking chair rocks away on its own on the porch

A solitary skull head in the mud is kicked to one side as my Death Row team emerge from a tunnel in front of a big campfire. I edited this entire piece together on a really old bit of Nero editing kit, and I had some fun doing it. I still have the out-takes somewhere including me going "Fuck it" after toe punting that skull which was heavier than it bloody looked.

We stride into town, acknowledging the locals who flee. The shot of Jonk turning and seeing us in the distance before throwing off his ironmonger leathers to burst in through the swinging Saloon doors to alert the Sheriff and the boys is a classic.

Dave turns over the table in fury after losing the card game just as Matty, who was in his early days wrestling as the Twisted Transvestite Deadly Nightshade, made his way down the stairs like a hideous Mae West. Dave slams him and sends him sprawling down the entire length of the bar in true Western fashion. That was great fun to film, sending Matty in his dress and tights at speed down this long bar like a slip n slide.

The bar keep, a young good looking lad called Rue who was showing incredible potential at the school, served up a shot and sent it sailing down the bar to an unseen recipient who turned out to be Skarlett decked out in a Sheriff's hat.

The next shot sees Skarlett rounding up her men and making their way one by one into the street.

Me, Phil and Sinders with his lantern, pass the Undertaker Helen who gives us a wry nod and tip of the hat.

The camera goes up high onto the balcony of the saloon for a wonderful bird's eye shot of the two sets of teams coming together for our first showdown.

As it runs along the train of eyes as a close-up for the calm before the storm, from the roof you see us both charge towards each other, and then a ground view of the charging Team Extreme bursting through the camera lens into a jarring blackout as the music comes to a phenomenal crescendo - leaving the viewer wondering the outcome.

I edited that piece together, and to this day it stands out as one of the very best wrestling promo videos of all time. It went viral at one stage and I'm incredibly proud of it. I went on to edit and produce three or four more mini movies to open the shows with on the big screen. None will top the Wild West one though.

Of course, an EWW day out wouldn't be the same would it without some sodding about. In the corner of the Saloon of course there was an Old Joanna - the piano. So of course, Greg was always the one to get naked in such team bonding scenarios and we thought we'd recreate the Terry Jones organ sketch from Monty Python.

Well, I'll tell you. Jonk with an eye for detail spotted a poo crumb to the left of his arse crack as Greg was merrily playing away on this out of tune piano that was missing a few keys with Jonk howling in the background . All of a sudden, the light went out in Greg's eyes as he realised this was probably going to be part of the video. As tempted as I was, it never saw the light of day. But that out of tune piano still haunts my dreams, and probably Greg's too.

The night itself came as we presented Survival of the Sickest to a packed out 800 strong crowd. It has always been a tradition in wrestling to get the crew together to go through the card and give a pep talk to your team. Not everyone does it, but we like to get everyone fired up backstage. I hate doing it, it's an arsehole on show day

38

when you've got people coming at you from all angles, there's only so much smiling my mouth wants to do in one day and it checks out pretty fast.

So I get the wife to do the team talk, she has the charm school about her when she wants too, so it's for the best.

After that we walked the team down a side tunnel and out on to the show floor away from the crowd in time to watch the house lights drop suddenly and hear the 'OOOH' from the crowd as the cinema screen lit up for the first time.

We watched together as they booed me, Phil and Sinders and a collective roar went up as the Sheriff is revealed as Skarlett. I looked over my shoulder through the darkness at Tarn and could see her bursting with excitement in the light of the giant screen. The video came to an end and got a gigantic roar from the crowd who knew they'd seen something a bit special. To say the atmosphere was electric doesn't do it justice, the noise from the people at the end of that set up the whole night and was the start of something very special for us at that venue. We really created magic there.

I wrestled my largest student in the undercard, Titan, or big Jonk to you. I came out with the woman who left Skarlett unconscious at our previous show and became the new EWW Women's Champion, Destiny.

Kat (Destiny) was an absolute heat machine and was the modern day Klondyke Kate for me.

Jayne, her real name and a dear friend of ours, wrestled all across the world through the 80's and 90's as 'Hell in Boots' Klondyke Kate. I watched her as a child and boy, did she have a presence - larger than life and a fantastic villain you feared and loathed in equal measure as soon as she came through the curtain. She really put women's wrestling on the map in Europe, there was nobody like her.

Now this girl Kat was in my mind the next best thing. A cracking wrestler, but she had that self-assured arrogance that made people hate her the moment she stepped through the curtain. Not to mention remarkable athleticism for a big girl, she could really put in a shift. I loved that, and of course it stood to reason that I'd have her in my corner to rile up Skarlett the team captain.

39

So anyway, the match was short, but punchy. Jonk at this point was still quite nervy around me when we worked each other. The first time at Wrestleforce in Harlow he'd stuttered on the finish, the second I knocked him out cold, and so third time lucky presumably.

Jonk was as a young wrestler everything you'd want in a student, humble, keen, took care of his appearance and although wasn't immediately a natural grappler, had a phenomenal aura. I kept on and on at him to use his height. I still fucking do. He's a corn-fed natural powerhouse of a boy who stands a legit 6'5. His father, a man in his 60's, can you believe dwarfs Jonk at nearly 6'8, and is one of the loveliest and softly spoken men I've ever met. Thank god.

So the boy has all the tools but was always reticent about putting a match together, no matter how hard I'd try and encourage him. We knew it was double duty tonight as we'd feature in the big main event too, so I wanted to keep it short and punchy. Nobody wants to see to giants out there for longer than ten minutes. It might look visibly impressive, but don't let's pretend it's going to be a technical masterclass. People want to see us tear lumps off each other.

Out came Destiny to present me to a chorus of boos, the place went up. I've always naturally felt more comfortable as a villain, it's so much fun and its definitely my happy place watching people's faces all screwed up in anger. Don't worry, I'm not acting here folks, I do genuinely want to punch your heads in. So much better than people wanting to touch you and throwing babies in the air don't you think?

Anyway, we did the eye-to-eye stare down. Well, almost eye to naval with this big white fuck. We did a test of strength and after I had him bump me around like a ping pong ball I took control of the match by taking him down by weakening the leg, all kinds of torturous leg and ankle locks to keep the big man grounded along with some skulduggery as I'd distract the referee to allow Destiny to get her licks in from the outside. All good stuff.

Titan was making his big comeback and given me a huge slam when all of a sudden, the lights went out. The building was in complete darkness and when they came back up Jynx, our resident Jester, was standing on the apron. He held his left hand up and from out of nowhere popped his signature cane and he broke it across Titans head, whilst sliding a steel chair to me under the bottom rope.

So now I'm standing waiting for the big giant to get to his feet, his back is facing me, and I know when he turns around it's lights out time. And POW!, the fucking chair folded over his head to perfection, it was a picture perfect shot. By god the guttural noise from the crowd was lovely as it sounded, like a rifle shot going off around the building. Titan dropped to his knees and of course I was disqualified. The man mountain left crumpled on the mat wearing the chair around his head still. There's a clip of it on YouTube somewhere, check it out, it was a doozy as they say.

I hauled ass out of there with Destiny and left the sleeping giant in the middle of the ring. But it had set up the tension for the main event rather perfectly.

And here we were. The Survival match with two teams of five pitted against each other. When one wrestler is pinned or counted out, they are eliminated and so on.

Coming into this match, Charlie Rage had been dethroned by Greg Stockwell as the new EWW champion and each member of each team had already wrestled their particular nemesis earlier on in the night, making this match even more important as it was literally the climax of what we'd been using as our big selling feuds for the last couple of years.

The villain faction was a very experienced team, me and four other generals who I knew I could count on to revel in this atmosphere and get the best out of it. Tarn had a harder time, both she and I knew that there were probably more than a few raised eyes in the locker room that she as 'bosses' wife' was going to be their team leader. Charlie was the most sceptical of all, and I always liked his honesty with us with things like that, as he'd just come out and say it rather than you having to hear it usually third hand. So Tarn had it all to do, and lots of people to convince, although me not being one of them because I wasn't prepared to budge on this one. We'd set the scene; it was time to dish up or shut up.

CHAPTER FOUR
BRING ON THE DANCING GIRLS

The crowd on this night were particularly rowdy, really up for it after that initial Wild West intro, they didn't stop until the final bell of the night.

There we were, the ten of us face to face. Skarlett and I started off to give the cameras the inevitable face off shot. I pie faced her and of course, queen of the angry faces as she is, came steaming in at me like a Jack Russell straight into a hard collar and elbow tie up and I took the arm with ease, teasing to snap it before forcing her into her corner to tag her brother Drake (Liam).

Liam was always far sharper technically than he was ever given credit for, he was prone to the old sloping shoulders if I wasn't there to kick him up the arse too, but a lovely kind-hearted lad who I honestly don't think ever believed he belonged with us. Despite the Prince of Punk gimmick and massive red mohican, he always cut an anxious figure backstage, which makes me think maybe I should've kicked him up the arse more. He needed that cattle prod.

Well, he got it here anyway as he leapt in over the top rope into my meatiest of clotheslines. BANJO! The usual dropkick, chops and torture ensued before feeding him to Jynx for some of Jases velvety offence.

Eventually after a nice meaty exchange in there with Dave (AWOL), Titan was set loose on me with a flurry of moves in retaliation for my party piece chair shot finale earlier in the evening. We both tumbled through the ropes and brawled into the crowd and got counted out. This left it 4 on 4.

Liam and Dave soon got eliminated leaving a rather one-sided Death Row vs Skarlett and Greg Stockwell.

Greg was suffering a bit with his confidence coming into this one too. When it's one of your own, and right before show time, it's the last thing you want to hear. Especially when you've just put your company's belt on him which at this point had 16 years of history.

I always put so much into these shows, to get 800 plus into an independent wrestling show consistently is no easy task and takes a lot of work, but we kept upping it every time, but a lot of people don't understand that when you possess a family atmosphere behind the scenes, you inadvertently end up taking on far more than that - so be warned future promoters out there who want to run shows with their own home grown students. You're like Mother, Father, Teacher, mentor, Soldier, Sailor....you get the fucking idea.

And in the end you run out of emotional plasters for these kids, each of whom can come with their individual needs, emotions and insecurities.

Let me just tell you this while it's on my mind now. It took me years and years to build a happy team at EWW, we had Awards nights at my friend's strip club, cracking little set up that was down in the cave in Hastings, and all kinds of get togethers to keep our bond tight and the home fires burning. Tarn was running her business, Skarlett's in Battle, a charming little coffee and bespoke cake business. She'd started out working at home and built to having her own premises and staff, having invented several concoctions that went on to get featured in LadBible and various other social publishers who were known for viral videos. With that, her little shop in Battle became a real destination for people who were travelling from all across the country to try these berserk Willy Wonka-esque delights. She went on to run that place for 7 years and luckily decided she fancied getting her qualifications as a Personal Trainer about three months before the Covid situation hit. Talk about timing.

But anyway, we'd have group meets in her shop and social gatherings to bond the team. It was certainly a very social time. The way I saw it, now and again you get a bad apple in the bowl, and you don't know it's bad until it's started to affect the others, we'd weeded out people like Kerry Cabrero for instance, someone who used to try and intimidate trainees.

These people sometimes go under the radar because trainees didn't feel it was their place to speak up, so the slime goes under the radar. Over the years, I'd also seen that there were so many locker rooms across Europe that were rife with scandal, 'he said/she said' and brimming tension so much that it ends up spilling out into the product. Very messy. I had spent several years at different times in EWW sitting back and watching my product to see how it could be improved. You can't force it, but you can foster it, and always build to what can eventually become a family environment.

But anyway, back to dear old Greg. It had happened before that, just when I was about to give someone a big push and run my show around somebody I believed in, they would then crumble. I could see it happening here. Greg had admitted he was nervous about it and would get himself in such a state before even training he would be sick. I remember him telling me this via a text message. I was furious. I had done nothing but bring him into my world and never been anything other than honest with him. Not only that, but I'd watched him go from being an anxious young lad riddled with Tourette's syndrome and grow into a handsome and confident guy with the world at his feet. It was enormously frustrating for me.

Granted he was my oldest student from Oxfordshire and had the longest journey of all mileage wise and yes, I've been a hard task master in my time, but other than the occasional 'hair dryer' scream up I've never given any of my students reason to fear training with me. The day I don't say a word to you is the day I have stopped caring. But I could tell that from this message, and from his body language at recent shows, that he was talking himself out of wrestling. You just know, and I'd seen people do it before, and unfortunately, he had a partner who would spitefully say things about his 'fake fighting' and I think it had chipped away at him. As I said in my last book, the amount of talent I'd seen disappear over the years because of resentful partners was up in the dozens. You can come to me with all the stories in the world, but as my old mate Jerry would say, "Don't piss on my shoes and tell me it's raining."

Back to the match though - it's not looking good for Team Extreme. Skarlett and Stockwell are facing Rage, Jynx, Exodus and Rage.

Skarlett had a superb chemistry with Rage, even though Charlie was sceptical about the inter-gender thing, I think when he went toe to toe with her, he realised that he was wrong. She rolled him up just as he appeared to have got the upper hand and the crowd were out of their seats it was fantastic. But just like every good thriller, they were about to have the rug pulled out from under them, as Greg was tagged in. Rather than being the house on fire and peeling off shots left and right, he was bumping into people and appeared bewildered and lost. I was watching this on the big screen from backstage and my mouth was dry, if ever there was a time I wanted to recreate the Mr Miyagi moment and nod to him that everything was alright and for him to come good, it was now. But it really wasn't.

He hit the ropes when faced with Jynx and Exodus, knocking Skarlett off the apron, he then stood and faced both men and was the epitome of a rabbit staring down a thundering juggernaut as he for some reason unbeknownst to everyone, suddenly remembered his fallen partner, turned, and called out 'Tarn?!?!'

It's pro wrestling. We have our gimmicks. If my opponent called me 'Stu' in front of hundreds of fans, I'd slap the taste out of his mouth.

The worst bit here was the crowd went completely silent, and it broke up the drama that had been built. Exodus and Jynx put Greg away with a beautiful but savage double choke slam and that was that. It was now three on one.

I know some people didn't agree that I'd made Tarnya the general of this match, and as I watched this beautiful angle come to an end, I could see it unravelling before my eyes into what is known in the industry as a 'cluster fuck'.

However, she scooted into the ring, stood, and the fear on her face surrounded by these three top heavyweights in British wrestling soon turned to anger, and in doing so the crowd rose with her in belief that she could do this. The noise, thank fuck, was again deafening. She managed to take the match by the scruff with these lads now left in the ring.

She spun like a dervish peeling off savage forearms to them, and as they'd regain balance she used cunning and speed to out manoeuvre them, There was a clothesline to Jynx over the top rope, a flying hurricane-rana to Exodus where she looked like Wonder Woman, her red hair spinning through the air like a helicopter

46

propeller, sending the big giant through the air too. Until finally Philip Bateman was there to put the brakes on the proceedings with a kick to her face and the short-lived comeback was over. It was exhilarating to watch and thankfully these four in the ring had saved this match, I was especially proud of Tarn here as her wild eyes, and facial expressions are quite literally second to none, and she had kids and adults believing in her. It's well worth a watch I can tell you.

But here she was, now at the mercy of Death Row who dispatched her lifeless body with ease, each of them performing their finisher on her, and the final blow being Jynx, soaring from the top rope bringing the curtain down on this feud. Death Row had won.

As they circled her like vultures, I now made my way out through the curtain to celebrate with my teammates, a certain sound of dread came from the audience as if they were about to witness a crucifixion. Bateman and Exodus held her up as Jynx presented Skarlett to me as if to say "Finish her off".

With that I spun, gave Jynx a back elbow leaving him stunned, left and right quick-fire punches to Bateman and Exodus before Jynx left me sprawling with a kidney punch. The crowd were back up on their feet, as after two years I'd come to rescue Skarlett, giving notice to Death Row.

Of course, the locker room emptied with Titan, Awol, Drake, Skarlett and I all hugging, people threw babies in the air and everyone went home happy. The outside of the ring was now swarming with kids banging on the apron, so many had run up to greet us I couldn't see how we were ever going to get out of there. It was a raging success. An incredible feeling. It's never a perfect show, but this was as close to one as I'd ever felt, but there's always something that keeps me grounded after the show and this time it was that Greg had come in as a star and was leaving looking like a lost kid.

In times like these I find it's like being the Goalkeeper in a game of Football. Nobody remembers all the saves; they only remember the shots you let past you. There was no repairing the lad.

Charlie and I did a few more tags as Death Row for various promoters and met our old foes the Hooligans, the Knight brothers, for the last time in what was always a hard hitter. We always loved working each other as it was like being back at school again - having a tear up and a beer after. There are never any hard feelings with those two boys as they always got the job done, made it look good and had a bloody good time doing it. What more could you ask for really?

I was about to drop the Wrestleforce title having won it only a couple of shows before. I always loved doing Charlie's shows, the best ones were always at the Harlow Playhouse. I had done stuff for him in Birmingham, and I think Luton where I tagged with Jynx which I was really looking forward to, until I saw we were on with the Devils Playboys.

Brett could work and enjoyed a bit of a scrap, but wrestling Sam Knee was like trying to push water up hill. He was always eager to entertain, but equally always unable to oblige. The match was one of those where you just hope nobody has filmed it or put it on social media.

But the Playhouse was set up perfectly for his type of show which was like a carnival. Bless him, we'd turn up and he was already in the ring giving directions to the dancing girls, high kicking with them, the lot. He didn't give a single shit it was his show and he was micro managing himself into a frenzy.

On this occasion he had brought Charlie Haas over fresh from leaving WWE and was going up against him in the cage in the main event. Poor Haas was laid out on the bleachers right behind me, every now and again raising his head and mumbling "What the fucks going on?" as Charlie was spinning around and high kicking in the ring with these girls like a chorus line girl in Paris. He didn't give a shit that he had a whole team of wrestlers from all around the country sat in front of him wondering what they were doing that night, he was in the moment. Bloody funny it was.

I'll never forget Gary Van Der Horne from Lucha Britannia who was a referee that night coming up to me and saying "They should call this Baffle Force".

The gimmick that night was my Heavyweight title could change hands all night long, so I basically had to hold onto it for the length of the evening and was set for a singles match with, I think Greg Burridge also from Lucha Britannia. Whoever won the belt would have to keep their eyes in the back of their head all night as an array of wrestlers and officials would be scrambling to try and win the belt over the duration of the evening. Or should I say, over the space of some hastily put together video sequences that would be played to the crowd on the big screen.

Say what you like about old Charlie though, but I loved his ideas. I didn't always like being a part of them myself though. Like I said before, doing fucking car chases through Essex at midnight and fighting through pubs whilst recovering from pneumonia is fucking exhausting, but his enthusiasm was such that it was hard to say no to the bugger. The one thing I did say no to was when he did a run of shows called TonteMania at a nightclub in Central London called Tonteria that he had a contract for.

There was no ring, and much like the bar fight wrestling that has become popular in the States, this was an early pre cursor for it. He'd have stars like Johnny Storm, Jody Fleisch and Flatliner (who I believe was dressed as the Abominable Snowman) fighting through this swanky nightclub and often out into Oxford Street. I kid you not. He phoned me up and said, "Oh mate come on it's a right laugh I promise you'll love it". Not a fucking chance my old friend, I'd be on the six o'clock news the next night for stoving in some punters, I could see the headlines.

He had his fixations with people did old Charlie, and he had one with a lad who was brand new in the business called Paul Synott. A Canadian kid, a decent machine body, and by that, I mean not a body built with many free weights. To me he looked like someone had photo shopped Conan O' Brien's head onto a Muscle and Fitness model's body. He had all the charisma of toast.

So I'm cool and ready for my match, and Charlie asks me to get in the ring. Synott is already in there. Charlie said, "Alright Stu so what's going to happen is the lights are going out and this cloaked figure is going to appear and smash a chair across your back and it'll be Paul."

Paul is standing slightly behind my left shoulder, completely vacant, and Charlie hands him a chair.

Now I thought to myself knowing Charlie's penchant for rehearsal, he's going to get this ginger muppet to practice hitting me isn't he. Surely not?

He said, "Here Paul just pretend you're going to whack Stu".

I said, "Have you done this before?"

To which he replied he hadn't. So I said, "Ok, well in your mind show me where you're going to aim for?"

With that he slowly swung the chair and stopped with the corner of the back rest at my temple!

I turned to him and said, "Now if you hit me there, I'm going to knock your fucking teeth out."

There was a nervous laugh from Charlie who then showed him exactly how to lay in a chair shot so as not to make either of us look stupid.

He'd already made the fatal mistake of saying to a handful of other wrestlers who were sitting in the bleachers, and in earshot of Tarn, "Why even bother having a women's match on the card, it takes up a spot for the guys"

She told me about this and she seemed remarkably calm, which took me by surprise. Big Jonk was on in the early part of the show with Synott and came backstage and said "Fuck me that geezers gear stunk of Oestrogeny women's piss."

Ah, that explained it!

I don't remember much about the match itself. I remember the Synott putting in the lightest chair shot across my back that would've struggled to have popped a zit, and then an onslaught of wrestlers who I'd never seen in my life pile on top of me, some had masks, I think one had a fucking Sombrero on. It was a right old panto. The bottom one of which was now apparently the new Champion, and they all ran off chasing him. I've no idea if I was meant to be giving chase at this point and stood there facing the audience. So much for going out on my shield, I'd just been pinned by the fucking Anthill Mob who'd all now done a runner.

Other than a bit of a punch up run in with Haas in the cage at the grand finale, that was me done with Wrestleforce. As happy as I'd been doing Charlie's shows, I didn't fancy doing any more, and this had left me with very little room to do anything else there even if I had. I'd done brawls through bars and car chase skits for videos for him at 1am on a winters night with pneumonia for fucks sake, I'd sat and watched patiently as he'd be high kicking with the chorus girls wondering exactly what my life was all about, but he was a good pal and always funny and I felt that if I did any more it would test our friendship as I was growing a bit tired, and with anything, as anyone who knows me will attest to, when that happens, I take it home - I'm done.

In the meantime, we did have a last booking together as Death Row. WAW had a huge new venue, Epic Studios in Norwich where they used to film the Trisha show. I'd done a show for them there where they'd stuck me in a Rumble and had me as the new recruit for their villain gang, The Midas Stable. I came in and beat the living Christ out of everyone left in there. I felt like fucking Gulliver in Lilliput behind the curtain before I went out, all these funny wrestlers of all shapes and sizes coming up and saying, "What do you want us to do Dominator".

I said, "Just run at me one at a time guys, you'll figure the rest out."

Sure enough they did, and were met with an array of fists, forearms and boots and bodies were sailing over the top rope like Lemmings off a cliff edge. But the show after that Death Row had our final match together as a tag team.

We'd been all over the place together, around the UK and France, and he was a great tag partner was Charlie, he looked the part and could really turn it on in there, we were a fearsome looking duo when we came out and made everyone else look rather small.

On this occasion we had a four-way tag match for the RQW tag titles. It was us versus the Army of Two (Aaron Sharp and Scott Fusion) the Metalheads, two lads who's names I forget but had the face paint and spikes and were like a poundshop version of us, so we made a bee line for those two, and the Bourne Stars (Joey Ozborne and Mitchell Starr).

On paper another cluster fuck. But it wasn't bad at all. Charlie and I dominated the opening, just keeping the Metalheads in the ring, peppering them with strikes, slams, dropkicks and pump handle slams, slinging them about like bin bags while the other two teams who'd been puffing their chests out on the entrances all of a sudden became a bit diminutive and looked like all of a sudden they didn't want to be there.

Eventually the Army of Two were tagged in, we did a stare down with them when I felt an almighty rabbit punch connect with the back of my neck, I saw stars for a few seconds. I knew the Metalheads had come in again to blindside us, and it was one of them. The one I got hold of got a right hook and two uppercuts and he was done. Charlie carried on the brawl at ringside as I did a two and fro with Aaron Sharpe. I was always left baffled with him, he was a nice lad, came into wrestling after working as a local doorman in the lively Norwich city centre, but not big on charisma which I think probably let him down despite the fact he could obviously work well, I never really thought he truly connected with the audience despite trying his best. Him and Fusion at least looked the part though and took the job seriously.

Anyway, I gave Aaron the dreaded sit down splash after he went for a sunset flip on me over the top rope. After that Charlie and I fixed our attention again on those two turds the Metalheads and beat them silly all the way backstage leaving the floor clear for the other two teams. Of course, we were counted out but stayed strong and it was the Army of Two who won the titles. All in all it was a cracking match that had a bit of everything.

After this was the big one. Ricky Knight, head of the Knight family and leader of the WAW revolution, had decided to call it a day after three decades of wrestling and he was hanging up his boots, and this was his retirement show. He called me up eager for me to be a part of this massive event and of course I wouldn't miss this one. Ricky Knight was there for my start in the business back in 1994, and I would move heaven and earth to be there for his final match.

I'd been working quite a lot for HEW, run out of Essex by Sam Knee and Brett Meadows. I had some great, and not so great, times there. One of my favourites was a chain match with Scott Fusion where we were both chained together, and the winner was the first to touch all four corner pads.

Scott had said to me backstage "A few of the WAW lot laughed when they heard I was going on with you, but I'm looking forward to it."

I didn't know how to take that, was he saying that they were disrespecting me, or that it was his way of telling me that he wasn't scared of me? It fucking aggravated me either way.

Wasn't a bad match though. He got a straight right to the chops from the outside which Brett always said was one of the funniest things he'd ever seen. Other than that we worked a solid match and I can't remember who won, for the sake of the book let's say it was me. You have to pace yourself with those chain matches, they're very limiting but, if you play it right, you can build a great story and tension with it. I think we did that.

In stark contrast the worst I ever had for HEW was with Charlie and I against the owners themselves Brett and Sam who were the Devils Playboys. Talk about oil and water, we did not mix well at all, it had all the grace of a monkey fucking a roller skate.

By god it was bad. Brett was a funny guy and a big ribber but didn't like it much if he got it back. He was a good-looking chap, long hair and always did a good job on his devilish face paint, and he could work too. Sam on the other hand was a sweet lad but had not a clue in the ring, despite having thousands of matches, he never improved. He had a lot of demons did Sam, none of them good ones.

We did our best with Sam and Brett. I could always work with Brett, but Sam, he'd just fold like a deckchair and slump in a corner or become a complete sandbag and make even your finest offence look like shit. It was painful. You'd end up wasting your own energy trying to move him around it was like having the last dance of the night with the biggest and most pissed girl on the dance floor.

I remember going to the back and saying "Fuck me", thinking there was nobody there.

Sweet Saraya was there crumpled on the floor laughing with tears streaming down her face saying, "Oh babe". She'd seen the whole awful spectacle. I've had a few bad ones with awkward opponents, but that was the worst for me hands down.

We worked quite a few matches for HEW as I mentioned in the last book, some great feuds, Skarlett Vs Saraya, and Death Row Vs The UK Hooligans (Zak and Roy Knight) good old punch ups they were, but in the end after Charlie wanted to hang his boots up, and we shall get to that part shortly, I didn't fancy the journeys over to Essex and we turned any further bookings down.

I went into Ricky Knight's retirement night at Epic Studios as part of Team HEW and was now teaming with my former foes, Sam and Brett. We were in another four way six man tag against Team Major League comprised of PN News, Doug Williams and Luke Hawx, Team Old School which   was Blondie Barrett, one of the nicest fellas in the business in my opinion, Steve Quintain and Bash, and the Army of Three which was Fusion, Sharpe and joined by Sam Slam, who I always thought was excellent, jacked and could shift in the ring too. I don't know why he never got signed by any of the big American companies, he was as good as Paul Burchill when he was in his prime, they were very similar.

12 men around the ring. Chaos again. I was in there for all of two minutes in total I think, first with Sam Slam and then Bash, there was no point vying to get your shit in with 10 other bodies stood on the apron, all the other lads so keen to be seen and try and outdo each other, even some of the veterans. You're getting your fee regardless and in a match like that you're lost in the shuffle, and my entrance on that night as usual was stronger than anyone else's. Nobody was going to see what you were doing in there amongst a mass of humanity unless you were in the final two, and we weren't, so I did my bit and that was that.

Team HEW were the first eliminated after Bash pinned Sam Knee, so it was no disappointment. A very easy pay day with no sweat broken and of course I got to be on my old mate Ricky's last show. Although of course much like George Foreman and Roddy Piper and many others before him, it proved not to be his retirement in the end. Pro wrestlers are an even funnier breed than anyone else in that respect. We're not guaranteed gigantic pay days and packed to the rafters events at the MGM Grand in Las Vegas like pro boxers, but the lure is just as powerful even if the lira maybe isn't.

In fact, it doesn't matter who you are, we've done shows with EWW where some of my childhood heroes who've been in the area have just turned up, to soak it all up again and have a laugh with the boys. The likes of Scrubber Daly, Mal Sanders, Nigel Hanmore and legendary European ref who's sadly no longer with us, Mal Mason, were often backstage at our shows. And let's face it, these guys did it when it was as much a staple of British life as Fish and Chips. Cauliflower ears, the lot, not a vape pen or a prewritten script in sight. It's in your blood, and there it shall remain. But on this occasion, we were in front of well over a thousand screaming punters that night and it was a big atmosphere. We were there for Ricky Knight.

Not too long after this I got a call from Charlie Rage. He'd had a heart attack and was in hospital for stents. I couldn't believe it. He sounded remarkably chipper and was mightily relieved. He used to be a drinker and enjoyed the party life and burning the candle both ends to extremes, and this was the wakeup call he needed. He was a tireless workaholic and had a deep fire burning in him that lad, that couldn't be extinguished. Whatever he did, he did obsessively. He came from quite a strict Arabic family with a crackers work ethic, I've not seen anything like it, he was a tornado of ideas.

He had a security business and was always travelling and had these hobbies that bordered on lunacy. I remember us in the locker room at HEW once and he'd built a fucking go kart track in the back of his house and had all these carts he'd painted up like Mario Kart on the Nintendo, but actual human size. He was so excited to tell me about it. Then it was paintballing, then making monster trucks with all these crazy gadgets. It was like a mad world he lived in at 100mph. But he was a great tag partner, and I had some crazy fun times with him.

When I had pneumonia for the first time, he came to visit me and insisted he and his partner Ruta, this incredibly tall Latvian girl, took Tarn and I out for dinner and then we all went Salsa dancing, which was his new obsession. Of course it fucking was. I was fucking ill, but he wouldn't hear of it. Off we went and he was teaching Tarn and I fucking Salsa whether we wanted to or not. He was bonkers, but I loved his chaotic fervour. There he was all suited up spinning around on the dance floor and kept looking over at me nodding as if to say "This is the fucking bollocks isn't' it mate, can you believe your life has been without this up until now."

Having been with us at EWW for quite a while where he had previously been our Champion, after some time recuperating Charlie said he wanted to go out on a high and retire on our show. When anyone wants to retire on your promotions turf it's an incredible honour no matter who it is, that person has travelled a hard road and is laying their hat down in front of your people. It's a big deal and I knew what we had to do, and we had a few months to prepare it.

CHAPTER FIVE
BLAZE OF GLORY

In the meantime we travelled again to Belgium and France where I'd done a couple of shows for a promotion over there. Tarn again defended her HEW Women's title which she'd won in Essex, and I wrestled as part of a six man tag main event on at least one of those shows. We'd get brought in to work a match, no angle, just boom here we are, hello, and goodbye back on the ferry again and then off to change the Euros at the bank. It was fun for a few years going back and doing the odd European gig, I was totally doing it for Tarn though, to get her a bit more experience and if I could get one of my other students on the shows then I'd do that too, like taking Greg over to France, despite his berserk driving up these old French side streets on the wrong side of the road. It felt like we were in those old soft focused romantic Renault Clio adverts on the old cobbled streets.

"Nicole?!"

"Papa!" Va va vooom splat!! Greg's just ran over fucking Papa!!!!!!!

The European shows were easy, especially if I didn't have to be main event as I wasn't expected to do all the extreme shenanigans we did in the late nineties like chair shots, table spots or fireballs, none of the old daft routine, as long as someone got a hiding, they were happy with that.

We'd been working for the Knight family at WAW quite a while by now and AWOL and I were getting a following as a hard-hitting tag team, often pitted against younger high fliers or local favourites like Kip Sabian and Brad Slayer or The Essex Boys, either that or they'd put us in other spots on the card where they needed a couple of hard hitters. They enjoyed a punch up in Norwich as I said last time around, my god did they. I can't remember too many occasions where there wasn't a melee of some kind with people fighting all over the place. I think it must've been like a call back to the older times in the nineties when the Corn Exchange was in full swing, the audience loved getting stuck in and it was always a punch up guaranteed.

Great fun all round. I think it must've been as close to a UK version of the World Class territory where the local sons were top of the bill and the crowd heavily believed in everything they were served up.

I'd already had a few lads tell me they'd be waiting for me in the car park at a show in Wymondham, clamouring to get my attention the whole fucking match. So at the end of the match I went over and said "Let's not wait till after, lets fucking have it now you thick cunts". Never saw them again, but in the nineties they'd have been waiting for sure. They didn't care up in Norwich. It's the only place I've ever seen on a Friday night with doorman at the Newsagents. I kid you not.

Skarlett however was competing on the sister brand of WAW called Bellatrix which were often the night before on the Friday. These as I mentioned in the previous book were the brainchild of Saraya Knight, and Tarn had got a huge following up there in Norwich with her new style of aggression and submission grappling that I was introducing her to at the Academy. She was becoming very natural at ground combat now, which is honestly something I never thought I'd see. She showed bugger all interest in grappling at first and was just a dive spot performer from what I could ascertain. Every single match I'd take her too whether it was NCW, HEW, WAW or some of the earlier shows I saw her on, she made me worried sick with her reckless style. If you're of a certain age, like me, you'll remember an old black and white action show on early Saturday morning telly called 'King of the Rocket Men'. He would often build up to some spectacular finale and end up smashing clumsily through a building or into an aeroplane to stop the villain. Rather than heroic, it looked fucking painful on his behalf leaving him in a crumpled heap.

Tarn was the King of the Rocket men to start with. Used to scare the fuck out of me it did watching her performances, physically capable but it was as if she wasn't physically in control of her own body parts and was being controlled by some lunatic with a remote control.

Skarlett had been on a run of matches with some great talent from around Europe and the American female promotion Shimmer, and she'd been a safe pair of hands for the Bellatrix brand in all of these and caught the eye of a lot of other promoters on hand.

One of these nights we were working at The Talk in Norwich, a real raw old nightclub but a good loud wrestling venue.

By the way, it must be noted that I had my own tradition I vehemently upheld at this venue. The WAW do like nothing better than a good old booze up, and so after the shows fans and wrestlers would always come together and we'd enjoy some after show beers. Always nice seeing fans from around Europe and some old friends.

The lads from Ring Wars, who were an online wrestling fan site, were always there, Ben Roberts and his partner in crime Ricky Kempster, two nice rotund and amiable fans of the grappling game who often came to our EWW shows and promoted us.

Now for the last year Ben had obviously been watching the old Peaky Blinders and got himself one of those silly hats that townies who fancy themselves as Game Keepers wear. I had a passion for snatching this off his head and it made a beautiful Frisbee which I'd send soaring into the light fittings. A cheer would go up and off he'd run bless him to try and find his silly Squeaky Blinders hat.

Anyway, he eventually got smart to this and pulled it down tight onto his little head so I couldn't snatch it so easily. So instead, I had to make do with setting him on fire. I'd go in for a hug just as we were about to leave and light the back of his hair with my lighter. I'd hold us there just long enough for it to smell and then let go as he'd be spinning like a dog chasing his tail and calling me no end of cunts. I got away with that at least three times. The last one he got thrown out of the venue for smoking as he insisted to deaf ears "NO, THAT CUNT SET ME ON FIRE!!"

It turned out a few years later that Ben was quite the sleaze merchant and had been sending pictures of his crooked little meat snack to various female fans. Perhaps setting him on fire was the right thing to do all along.

Anyway, AWOL and I were representing EWW in a 'Tag team Rumble' for the WAW tag titles which were combined with the French ECTA tag titles at the time. A peculiar addition to the usual Battle Royal rules, it had a couple of referees outside the ring, and nobody had a fucking clue what was going on. Jimmy Ocean from the Superflys was one of the referees. Dave (AWOL) and I were the first team in the ring followed by the Essex Boys. Then every two minutes another team would come in until only one was left. Anyway, Jimmy comes up to me as I'm out the back of the venue and with his gravelly voice said, "Right then bud, what are we doing?"

"I was waiting for you to tell me Jimmy"

"Oh bollocks"

Yeah, it all went a bit like that. We started it off with The Essex Boys, Paul Tyrell my fellow Skullkrusher, and filthy low life Phil Powers and we traded off and had a punch up. Dave loves getting stuck in so was in his element. Two minutes pass and into the match came the two lads we'd had a feud with, Special Edition, who took us all out with two beautifully synchronised drop-kicks from the opposing top ropes. Followed by my old mate Ruffneck, always good to see his big daft face in the ring, it's an easy target and he does insist on running gleefully at full tilt into my fist...So to speak.

Anyway, he was there with his tag partner followed by the Bourne Stars, Lee Mitchell and Joey Ozborne.

Now, Lee Mitchell is a lovely kid, but on this occasion forgot to sell for me this time, and to me, when the Knights ask you to be an unstoppable monster and a pretty blonde lad stands toe to toe with you not registering strikes, or on this occasion, an eye rake, then it causes me to give him a flurry of very real looking peacemakers, which made his head look like a Nik Nak. He had no trouble selling those.

After headbutting my way through this match and launching a few bodies out of the ring, some of whom were reluctant to go so soon, but had little choice, it was time to make way.

Kip Sabian wiped AWOL and I out with a lovely plancha dive from the top to the outside and all four of us brawled to the back for the inevitable double count out. No idea who won the match in the end. Not us, so who cares.

Tarn was in a match the following night at the same venue for Bellatrix against a much smaller opponent, Shax. Skarlett was getting a mixture of babyface and villain heat from the crowd, the Skarlett gimmick and goth bad ass really appealed to the females who supported the female shows. She'd been working with a lot of females who had more experience than her and she rose to the occasion every time. The Bellatrix shows were always on the night after the male roster and the girls had something to prove and therefore were always so good to watch because they would tear lumps out of each other, it was a fantastic advert for European women's wrestling the Bellatrix product. There were other female promotions in the UK but often had a nasty undercurrent of sleaze running throughout and that was definitely not the case here. We would only ever do business with the Knights.

So Shax was visibly nervous going up against Skarlett who kept on weakening her left arm in the early going with Shax reluctant to really ever get going. Of course, Skarlett took advantage of this and dominated her for the opening minutes with a mix of strikes and nasty submissions. She polished Shax off pretty fast after a short comeback and made her tap out with her finisher the Skarlett's Web which is a beautiful move made even better by Tarns ability to bridge into an almost contortionist position thus stretching her opponent further.

The British Women's champion at the time was Chanel who was good little worker from Manchester. She'd been the champ for quite a while, and it had been announced that she wouldn't be defending her title that night due to illness.

At the interval Saraya came over to grab Dave and I and asked if we could go backstage. Getting asked to go backstage is never normally a good thing and the first thing that went through my mind was that Tarn was injured, although I couldn't figure out how as she'd breezed through the match.

So we get backstage and Saraya turned to me and said "We haven't told anyone yet but we're putting the belt on Tarn."

I was chuffed to pieces because I knew how hard Tarn had worked for Bellatrix. She believed in the product and had an affinity with Julia Knight. It was a nice touch to drop it on her too as she had no time to prepare for it and that was when she was at her best, Julia tapped into that nicely.

And so Chanel Vs Skarlett was happening. Chanel had Kip Sabian and Brad Slayer as her corner men that night. They liked to do things in an old school manner in Norwich when it came to the title matches. Corner men, national anthems, the lot.

61

It was always an occasion. Tarn wanted Dave and me to be her corner men, so we were stood backstage at this point not dressed for the occasion like two spare pricks at a wedding.

The match went ahead with Chanel looking pensive and vulnerable and so the crowd were right on her side, it was set up perfectly, that coupled with the fact that Dave and I had been working matches against Chanel's two corner men Special Edition, so it was kicking off outside the ring too.

The crowd were super-hot. The British title matches were traditionally done in rounds too and this one was best of three falls.

After an altercation with Special Edition, Chanel rolled Skarlett up for the first fall in only 5 seconds, the crowd went crazy.

After a super stiff exchange of forearm shots between the two, with Chanel looking absolutely battered it was very clear that the training Skarlett had been putting in at the Academy was paying off. Chanel was breathing hard, and despite being ill didn't have anywhere near the same engine as Tarn. She got the equalising fall with the Skarletts Web submission.

It was Round three or four now and Chanel was propped up in her corner, mascara running and only the ropes were holding her up as from across the ring, Skarlett was beckoning to her as AWOL and I goaded the lot of them.

She lasted seconds of that next round as she walked into a barrage of rising knees and fell to the Axe kick to the back of her head. Skarlett pinned her to become their new British Champion. AWOL and I celebrated in the ring with the new champ, it was so loud in there now, it felt great.

Saraya came out to help Chanel from the ring and got on the microphone to try and re-direct a bit of shine back to Chanel, but we stayed put and as was usual when we were in Norwich. We created a storm, beat people up, and on this occasion, took the gold home.

To me, Tarn deserved this a much as any of her belts, it was earned the hard way, which is the right way in professional wrestling.

So many are quick to judge us as fakes, and over the years a lot of promotions have given way to tipping a nod and a wink to the crowd as if to acknowledge this. I fucking hate that. It's absolutely disrespectful, not to mention cowardly to cow tow to outsiders views when you've gone to the trouble of 'hopefully' honing your craft and fighting for your spot. This was literally a classic example of watching someone climb a ladder in a company, and climb it the hard way, having been given a hiding by the likes of Busty Keegan, to gaining the respect of all her peers as she studied the art of submission fighting and became the one girl that Julia Knight could always rely on.

And let's face facts, as any woman of note in wrestling around the globe will tell you, when Sweet Saraya is putting her money on certain talent she would usually make them earn it, and rightly so. A lot of the wrestling business had certainly got softer in many ways but making your talent fight for their spot is certainly something I respected in a world that was rapidly changing before my eyes, not all for the better either. But this one felt very good.

My old buddy Evo, my beloved English Bull Terrier who I'd had for 11 years passed away not long after this. That broke my heart. What a character he was. People used to cross the road to avoid us, which just goes to show how stupid people are, because he was genuinely the kindest dog I've ever known, an absolutely incredible example of his breed. Pure white, he was like a big old sock puppet, pure muscle and always in tip top shape, but was starting to get old. He had a heart murmur and walking was getting too much for him.

They have such stubbornness the English Bulls, and even as a young dog when living in the Cotswolds he'd refuse to walk certain ways or past stationary motorbikes. I'd have to carry him, his four stiff legs sticking out like a fucking deck chair.

But now he was really slowing up and would collapse when he'd come in from a short evening walk to the beach. His eyes would glaze over and he'd stiffen up and just topple sideways. We got so used to this that Tarn would be ready to catch him, it was like clockwork. We'd swaddle him in warm towels and he'd eventually come to and be right as rain, if not a little dazed. I had of course taken him to the vet to get checked out, but he was too old to be operated on and I knew it was something that would eventually take him.

Alas, this one night he didn't come to and just went at home, peacefully, and you can't really ask for more than that having had years and years of incredible journeys with him. Tarn and I cried our hearts out that night. He was such a character and loved by everyone who met him.

There was literally nothing he loved more than show day because of the amount of people who fussed him, and he knew he could sleep on so many shapes and sizes. From Bulk to Little Legs, to Berry, he slept on them all with a smile on his face, he loved when the wrestlers slept over, he had his pick of comfy giants to sleep on. He loved the wrestlers so much and they loved him. Apart from Flatliner who once stood with his clumsy great Doctor Martin wearing feet on Evo's paw, the next minute Chris is hopping around my kitchen screaming "Help, he's got me!!" with Evo hanging off his camouflage trousers like a Piranha fish. It was hilarious.

My old housemate in Oxford Tom and I used to partake in a little of the night puff. I remember Tom's first night there, we were both stoned out of our boxes and Evo was sat upright on a chair just staring him out. We were watching the Japanese horror 'The Ring' at the time. Tom turned to me and said "Chief, your dog's wigging me out bro".

The one story that always gets brought up though is when I had a house full of Americans after a show in Oxford. I had a huge, dare I say very 70's, glass topped low table that my father used to keep his record player on and all his vinyls underneath. I had it now and was using it as a retro coffee table. It really was from 1970's Germany in every way, brushed steel and glass. It met its fucking Waterloo here though in spectacular style.

We were all sitting around talking and then SMASH!, Evo had crawled under the bottom and emerged like a fucking shark through the glass, coffee and beer everywhere and his stupid bone head smiling in the middle of all of it. It scared the shit out of all of us. Christ alive it was like the bloody Jack Nicholson "Here's Johnny!" moment from The Shining. Bone headed hound!!

Rest in Peace my dear faithful sock puppet friend.

CHAPTER SIX
RAGE

It was our annual extravaganza Invasion of the Bodyslammers 4 and our main event was Dominator Vs Rage, former tag partners collide and the loser retires forever. So that was how we'd cover it.

I'd made it known that I was getting tired and had several nagging injuries including my right ankle which rolls constantly after being pinned and set incorrectly after a major car crash. It looks pretty bad at the best of times but flares up and causes me huge pain, especially after wrestling, and I think a lot of people were wondering if I was retiring.

Once again we packed Kings Venue to standing room only. I loved that venue, it was always rammed in there and incredible acoustics, everything you'd want on a big fight night. Obviously, the retirement match was top of the bill and there was a lot of nervous tension around. Especially from me as I was going on with one of my mates who'd had a bloody heart attack and wasn't exactly known for my sympathetic bedside manner when it came to wrestling matches.

The show was memorable for a few firsts, it was a packed-out card with the debut of my old pal, the scourge of Newcastle, Keith Colwill, and my childhood hero Danny Boy Collins. I'm glad I got that the right way round!

I absolutely idolised Danny when I was a kid, he did the lot and was a real life superhero to me with his flashing smile and death defying moves that would defeat the villains on Saturday afternoon television, I think he's the very first wrestler who really made me care, you know, as if you were watching your favourite football team in a cup final. I'd done several shows on the bill with him around the country, but it was a huge honour to have him here for EWW that night.

He'd done a seminar for me at my academy a couple of months prior to the show and was absolutely superb. Why other schools hadn't picked him up to teach more frequently I don't know. In my eyes there's nobody better to cast an eye over your students and spot what they need to sharpen and more importantly, show them how to do it.

Bear in mind that Danny at this stage was in his fifties and still possessed the agility, balance and speed of a man in his twenties, his seminar with us was quite literally a masterclass of the British style, which to me, people like he, Adrian, Jim Breaks, Fit Finlay, Marty Jones, and more recently Steve (William) Regal, made look so effortless.

To me there is something uniquely timeless about that style of grappling, it's honest and it looks real because it is. It's gratifyingly neat and tidy and to me is a real art form. It was pure joy for me to watch a man I'd literally idolised as a child teaching my students, just wonderful. If you're an aspiring wrestler then I'd highly recommend any young guys or girls who are reading this to study the man.

Anyway, I'd chosen one of my top students at the time, Joby, to go on with Danny, by way of a reward for his hard work. But he completely shit the bed and let me down and ended up missing the show entirely as his nerves got the better of him.

So instead a young lad called Jason Sensation went on with Danny. I wish I'd done things differently rather than use this as an attraction match, I should have brought Danny in for more bookings, but instead I put him on with Jason that night which was hasty to say the least, he was a very nice lad, but ended up breaking his wrist in a warm up that day. The match went ahead, and of course Danny covered everything like the true pro you'd expect, but it wasn't the big show piece I'd had in mind, it felt like it was snake bit from the get go. Although the huge Hastings crowd we had in that night gave the veteran a fantastic welcome.

Skarlett continued her rise through the ranks against Chuck Cyrus, a lad who was a good self-publicist but didn't ever seem to realise where his place was on the card. He would rather work on an outlaw, cheap arse village hall show and be top of the bill as opposed to mid card in front of a thousand people. That mentality is alive and well in British wrestling, and I'll never understand it as long as I live.

You get these wrestlers who go out there and try to kill themselves with ludicrous stunts to try and light up a crowd of 100 who wouldn't even raise an eyebrow to a fucking bomb going off, but put them in an arena with 800 to 1000 people and watch them try and hide in plain sight. It's an absolute fucking nonsense, and I see it all the time. It's the reason I have agents work with my guys and girls for each match as some people always looked at working for me as a night off because it was an 'easy crowd' who will pop for the smallest of things.

But the night was all about Charlie. A mate of mine who I'd been extremely close to and travelled all over the place with. We'd done television, caused havoc in France, raced cars around Essex and hung out together socially, he was and is a very fun guy to be around and is one of those rarest of individuals who can make me laugh.

I wanted to give him a great send off. He'd been the leader of Death Row, a faction who broke all the rules and had some of the loudest villain reactions we ever saw in EWW, Charlie and I had wrestled each other loads and knew each other's repertoire. This wasn't our best match, it didn't entirely click that night, but it meant the most of them all.

I was nervous because I knew how much was riding on it and obviously I was trying to constantly push the nagging reminder of Charlie's heart attack to the back of my mind, but every time I'd go through the match in my head, that would leap to the forefront of my thoughts and throw me off completely. Watching this back, I looked like a bit of a rabbit in the headlights. I had to look after my old pal here as opposed to the usual feeling that I was going to war which, as anyone who has been on with me will tell you, is exactly how it is for both parties.

We tied up hard and spent the first six minutes butting heads and meeting each other move for move like two big old stags in a field, neither giving an inch. Eventually the battle opened up when Charlie went to vault over the top of my head, but I caught his legs and threw him over the top to the outside. He liked that spot and did it well, and it always scared the shit out of the people in the first couple of rows.

I ended up taking the heat and I think probably sold my knee and allowed him to take advantage. I'd not been right physically since having pneumonia twice a year or so before this match, and my right lung was scarred up badly leaving me no spare gas in the tank at all.

I remember we did the 'three ring circus' routine where we had villains from the roster come and wipe me out mid match only to be chased off by their counterparts. I've always liked lots of action in my matches and no matter where it came from, I always found chaos to be the best ingredient to light up a crowd. Whether it was a brawling start, some interference in the middle or a wild west saloon brawl after the final bell, the best way to send them home happy and throwing babies in the air in delight was always to sprinkle chaos into the mix. Not only that, but it also took away from my shortcomings in this match and instead added a lovely bit of added drama.

First Jynx, who hit me with the magic disappearing cane, and then followed by Phil Bateman and Stockwell who had earlier in the night teased our newest creation, the Children of Eden.

In the nights earlier match we had our then Champion Stockwell relinquish his EWW title and becoming transfixed on a video we played on the giant video screen. This strays away somewhat from my match with Charlie, but it all comes together in the end, so do stay with me dear reader.

I had always been fascinated with Cults. Yes, I said Cults….and specifically mind control. From my earliest memories of Jonestown and the wicked story of what went down in Guyana with the poor souls from the Peoples Temple who perished. There were hundreds of men, women and children in the largest suicide pact in history, which was led by the charismatic leader the Reverend Jim Jones. I'd wanted to read about how this was possible, to pull so many people from all different walks of life on side.

Ever since EWW's inception back in 1998 we had always had a strong villain faction. During my early training Adrian Street always told me the same stories every day, and for fear of getting a hiding I'd always listen intently. But he'd always tell a wonderful story of Lancelot and how he'd go back to the Knights of the Round Table completely unharmed after easily vanquishing everything in his wake. Had there of course been no dragon of Corbenic in the story, would he have had his legendary status?

With no great villain, there will never be any great heroes. And for me, that is where modern wrestling has fallen very short.

However, I had this drummed into me at wrestling school so never made that mistake. Dead Souls, who although were undoubtedly a rather cool attraction with scantily clad women and live snakes, were very much the 'dark side' and of course we had Jody Fleisch, Fighting Spirit and Frankie Capone who were the good guys. It sold a lot of tickets when British wrestling was on its arse. You'll get a lot of people who will say that it wasn't, but I'm telling you it was like a fish flip flopping around in a puddle, and the cool new 'Attitude era' in America could never be replicated over here by the likes of Brian Dixon's crew who were knocking out the same tired old shit they'd been doing for years.

"And now the raffle ladies and gentlemen", hardly puts you in mind of fucking Madison Square Garden does it?

So much had changed overseas, but nothing had changed here. So we changed it. That's right, we did. Before the FWA, we were lighting up venues with pyros, dry ice and gadgets, and dragged British wrestling along into the modern era. We were despised by some, mocked by others, but we didn't give a shit, Jamie and I were unapologetic about our approach. Someone needed to rattle the cages, and we were the ones who had the bollocks to do something that would give the business a much-needed cattle prod.

Looking back at the shows, we didn't have the great HD cameras or editing facilities that you can even get on a smart phone these days, but if you watch our early exploits, you will see what I mean. Nobody did what we did - or even came close.

So, back to my point. The villains had to be that damn strong, and I'd tried to do a version of the Children of Eden early on called 'The League of Love'. The problem is, nobody who was in the League actually understood how to execute it and it looked like a bunch of silly sods who'd just painted themselves in glue and ran amok in a fancy dress shop.

With Rage now retiring we needed something that people could hang their hat on. And so I chose my old friend Phil Bedwell, aka Philip Bateman, who also was extremely well read when it came to studying Cults. I came up with the name, the Children of Eden, he came up with the imagery, and there was even a call back to the old Dead Souls faction with the triangle in the logo as it's the strongest shape of all with the most solid base.

But how would we drop it in.....?

After Phil's match on this night with Greg, the lights in the venue flickered on and off very briefly several times, throwing people off, not knowing if it was part of the show or not. Suddenly the video wall came alive with loud static over the speakers, I told the lad doing the sound to turn it up really loud. It was jarring. The old footage of Jim Jones came into view sitting casually before a reporter, "Lay down your burdens" he said. A quick cut to Charles Manson, followed by the insane smiling grin of Marshall Applewhite gazing down into the audience. All this along with whispers of Phil himself saying "Join us" which I dropped into the audio.

It was a dark and dangerous idea that could've met with some hostility, especially as we were running in this huge exhibition centre that doubled as a church on Sundays. I'd always enjoyed riding the waves of controversy and courting danger back in our early days, and other than the moment when Dominator turned on Skarlett, in my mind we hadn't really done enough to provoke the audience or shock anyone like I knew we could. This was very risky thought, but it worked, and more importantly, we got away with it.

The video only lasted about 50 seconds, if that, but every one of the 800 people in attendance were looking up at it. Our seed for the beginning of Eden was planted.

So back to my match with Rage. After a brief flurry of a comeback and a near pin fall, he laid me out and went to the top rope for his infamous Thunder-Sault. It always looked spectacular, he was a big lad old Charlie, but it was a picture perfect moonsault that he'd execute. I'd taken it from him many, many times, but he'd put on a little bit of timber, and he came down hard. Fuck me, I nearly shot a bum cigar into the fifth row like a torpedo. Christ, "stiff cunt" I thought. Actually I'm not entirely certain I didn't exclaim it out loud.

He went to the top again after not pinning me, I knew I had to have another one, and was so winded I just hoped this one might be easier. But alas, no. WHAM!, he laid me out like a fucking hammer on a braising steak.

He had called the finish, which I hadn't really been keen on but it was his match and so I went with it. He wanted to hit me with three of these, and on the third, I'd pop straight up and roll him up in a folding cradle as he was going to slam me.

Well, he hit the third, popped up to his feet, and I wasn't even on my feet as his heavy arse had laid me out like a kipper three times on the trot. Before I knew it, he was coming at me and I barely got my bearings before he folded himself into me and over we went for the cradle, which I hated personally, it looked like I was fighting a losing battle with a deck chair. But that was it, 1, 2, 3, he had gone out on his shield in true wrestling tradition, and I'd retired the Rage in somewhat clumsy style. The match went out on eventually on Sky TV too via WAW programming so a whole new audience got to witness that shit finish too.

As was always the way at the Hastings Centre the kids would rush to the front and surround the ring, banging their hands on the apron in delight, it was always a great end to the night seeing them swarm from their seats to show their adoration for their heroes. This night was no different as although Charlie had always been a top card villain in my EWW shows, the audience realised they were seeing something special, the end of a career - this was very real.

Charlie gave his last speech and bid farewell and was given a great send off, one which he was incredibly humbled by. And with that, he was done. He sold his wrestling ring, van, the lot. WrestleForce was now no longer his and what had been his life for so many years was now in the rear-view mirror. He was a fascinating and unusual chap, he was a mad keen hobbyist and if he had his eye on something, he'd devote everything to it. Like building the monster truck we went to France in, with every conceivable gadget inside it too. I hear from him occasionally, he's living in Gibraltar now, probably doing something barmy like building a Bond villain hideout for all I know.

We had so much fun making the mini movies that played on the giant screen as the lights would go down to herald the beginning of our shows. It always kept the audience completely focused on the theme we were trying to portray throughout, and it was also a kindly nod to new audience members.

We had now said goodbye to Death Row, and as is my tradition with EWW, when one faction dies out, they are re-spawned into another entity entirely. In this case, The Children of Eden.

I had brought Liam Dowe in to help with our writing, our meetings were sometimes reminiscent of our original meetings in the late nineties with Jamie and Josh and would spill over into complete tangents and piss ups. But for the most part we got some great stuff written and what was more remarkable was that we managed to execute it so well on film. I used to edit everything myself and as I said, the Wild West piece is to this day still the best one I ever did. Luckily nowadays I have a youthful and ambitious army of lunatics who put these things together for me, for which I'm ever so thankful. I'm more likely to Frisbee a fucking laptop out of the window these days rather than pretend to be content whilst hunched over the thing with doom etched on my brow, botching and swearing my way through another edit job.

In the meantime I was called by my old friend Ricky Knight who wanted us for a big new project his WAW company were involved with up in Norwich. It was to be a series of television shows called Epic Encounters, filmed at the famous television studios at Epic Studios where loads of famous television shows have been filmed over the years such as Knightmare and Loose Women.

It was a big project with a large financial backing, and they were bringing a lot of top tier American talent over for these events that would be taped over a whole weekend several times a year to eventually go out as one hour episodes.

Many companies had tried shots at television since Greg Dyke pulled the plug on World of Sport wrestling on ITV in 1988, and here for you dear reader is a short summary of the history of how British wrestling faired in the several attempts after,

In the nineties and early turn of the Millennium, most notably there was Satellite Wrestling which went out on Screensport, a low budget version of World of Sport and the Welsh speaking version Reslo. Jackie Pallo Jr had a very brief run on ITV in the early hours of the morning with WAW (not to be confused with the Norwich lot) which I think was taped over in Las Vegas. It was pretty awful stuff.

There was the Transatlantic Wrestling Challenge, also on ITV, which had a few stars from Hammerlock involved. And of course, the UWA with former WWF editor Andrew Martin and Dan Berlinka, which after a couple of promising episodes soon shot their bolt and sank without trace.

Then there was the Tommy Boyd show The King of England tournament which was known as Revival, and which I was a very small part of. It went out on the Bravo TV channel from Crystal Palace arena and was a huge event with Eddie Guerrero headlining.

Once again, the budget for this was enormous and again produced a fine one-off television event – but with literally nothing left over. Tommy Boyd was never heard from again. So, with this pretty awful track record I was really hopeful that this would be different.

CHAPTER SEVEN
CRITICAL MASS

At this point I'd just started the tag team Critical Mass with my student Jon Kocel aka Titan. Jon is a mountain of a man, a legit six foot five of Polish heritage with a fearsome reach and sharp but heavy features when angry that could curdle milk. Something rarely seen in someone so young.

Starting another tag team was something we'd been planning for a while and with injuries and pain starting to get the better of me, including a severe deterioration in my right ankle from a serious car crash many years ago where my foot was pinned together, it was harder and harder for me to maintain decent length matches and would be hobbling around on a swollen ankle for days after. A tag team with a younger partner would certainly benefit me. Or so I thought at the time. Poor old Jonk as we call him went from injury to injury, I've literally never seen someone with such bad luck - he could fall into a barrel of tits and come up sucking his thumb. Jonk is a self taught armourer. He was brought up by his father, as mentioned a giant himself, and he would put on Robert Taylor in Knights of the Round Table for Jonk at an early age and take him to every castle in the country. Jonk always wanted armour but could never afford it, so went to see a Blacksmith who told him that not only was it not possible, but there wasn't a hope in hell that he could ever make it. Walking away thinking "Fuck that" he set about making his own and hollowed out a dish in a log to beat steel in and brought hammers from old boys at car boot sales. He was 12. Now to me that shows some remarkable dedication and maturity. I was fiddling with my dick at 12 not trying to figure out how to make my dream a reality.

He is the only armourer in the world to be commissioned by royalty for a real Knight, Sir Nicholas Saunders in West Sussex, who died in the first half of the 1600's.

His reproduction of Saunders' stolen helmet is mounted directly above Saunders' tomb in Charlwood, over his body at the altar with his name on the plaque. He now restores originals and runs a college course teaching Blacksmiths the finer techniques. How's that for someone who was told a child "Nah, it'll never happen son", by basically some bitter old bastard who couldn't be bothered to pass on the knowledge.

To me, there was no greater likeness to the wrestling business that I started off in, and I tell you what, there's no greater fucking motivator than some jaded old sod telling you no, and getting off on watching the joy leave your eyes. It makes you want it more. And I always loved hearing how he'd written his own destiny, I love that.

So the plan was in place, we would become Critical Mass. Dominator and Titan, and Jonk would create fearsome armour helmets for our entrance. They had motionless pointed faces, mine had a heavy veil of chain mail down the back which fell across my shoulders, they were awesome pieces. I still have mine mounted on a mannequin head in our spare room, it's quite a piece.

When we came up with Critical Mass we knew we would be getting a lot of bookings as the tag team ranks in European wrestling were hardly brimming with real tag teams, and the ones who claimed to be giants were just lazy fat slobs who'd never had a real fight in their lives in all honesty, whereas Jonk and I were the real deal and a fearsome looking set up.

We did a whole bunch of bookings in our first year together for promotions up and down the country before we hit the road to do the Epic Studio shows for WAW. I wanted us to refine our look and matches as I didn't want us to be just known as brawlers, although that would probably be inevitable. There were a lot of people wanting to book us from Portsmouth to Scotland and not all of them were of interest to us because although it's a nice day out, quite frankly having just reached my forties, and without the benefit of wide eyed wonder that you have in your earlier years, the thought of driving up to Scotland and back in a day was up there with hacking your bollocks off with a rusty spoon.

We did shows for my old pal Brett Meadows and his promotion World War Wrestling which was, and is, a cracking promotion. Full of gimmicks, stories and production. I like to think that Brett was probably influenced by EWW in his time with me because he certainly had the same bombastic style of promoting and spent a lot of time in the editing room putting together cracking music videos and horror movie style promos, and we were really the only ones doing that. But WWW came along and were doing it very well and I enjoyed doing his shows.

I worked a lot of singles matches for them before Critical Mass came along, and although Brett wasn't enamoured with Jonks style, he thought we looked the bollocks and we did a run of shows with him up near Suffolk in singles and tags.

We did some shows in Portsmouth and Gosport for my old pal Flatliner. Chris Manns, the man behind Flatliner is another one of my band of merry men who are like Marmite, you love him or you hate him. It always seems to be the way with my pals and me. I think it's because we've never catered for the smart fan, the ones who sit on their hands and don't spend money, just a lot of time slating me and my pals because we're just big lugs who punch people in the face or get up to naughtiness. I've been unapologetic in the fact that me and EWW have always represented the freak show nature of pro wrestling from the 'olden days', and I know some people think its outdated and therefore no longer relevant, but to me pro wrestling has to be built that way, because there are so many legitimate fight shows in every big town in the country now, whether it's white collar boxing, MMA or a local kickboxing show, if you want to see that, more power to you, but when the circus is in town, everyone always knows about it don't they. The posters are garish and you see them everywhere you go. There's no awkwardly posed skinny lads in faux aggressive fighting stances, its high flying, explosions, people being shot out of fucking cannons. Wrestling should be the same, every freak and giant on the poster. I can see little Kevin have a fight outside the Dog and Duck on a Friday night for free for fucks sake, so why would I want to pay for it. That's why Kickboxing and MMA events can't touch us for numbers, they never have and they never will.

I've been packing houses out for years and years doing that with EWW, and we rarely do a house under 600 people. So I must be fucking doing something right.

Chris Manns, the Flatliner, has the same attitude. Well obviously. He looks like a classic old circus strongman with features and frame that bely his years. We've been firm friends for many, many years, and if you read my first book Simply the Beast you will know all about that.

85

Chris has probably divided opinion amongst wrestling fans more than anyone else in the last two decades. He knew he didn't have the ability to be a classic pro wrestler and instead opted to do comedy. And although a lot of people in the wrestling business say, "Funny don't make money", in his case, it does. He clears more merchandise than almost everyone, and families love him. And over the years he has come under attack because of some fairly high-profile pranks that have got him into trouble. But it's worth noting that he has done far more for the power of good than almost anyone I know in professional wrestling. From visiting sick kids in hospital, to organising events for under privileged people and to raising awareness of knife crime in his area of Gosport where he is the local celebrity. He can't leave his abode without someone stopping him. He's a walking advert for 80's nostalgia and pro wrestling with his giant chains, bandanas, the lot. If he's walking down the street in your town, you know wrestling is in town, and isn't that better than some little arse wipe who looks like they work at Halfords?? And the best bit about Chris is that he's never changed, and I like that about him, he really couldn't give a fuck what people think. But I want it putting out there what good he does for the community because there are some nasty, spiteful little arseholes in the wrestling business, more in the UK than anywhere else, who try and get him cancelled. And considering most of their friends are only in wrestling to hold dominion over young impressionable girls, is a bit fucking rich in my opinion.

So anyway, much digression here. Chris wanted to bring me and Jonk up as Critical Mass for some shows in the Portsmouth and Gosport area. If you stick Chris on the poster in Gosport then obviously it's going to be a sell-out show, so of course we were up for it.

Here's a couple of memorable moments from those shows. I was tagging with this enormous great ginger kid who was done up like Bruiser Brody in the fake furs and Viking get up. Don't remember his name but he was a softly spoken and gentle lad and looked great. Jonk was in a singles that night I think, and me and this kid were up against Flatliner and the UKs strongest man at the time - Rob Frampton. I'd met Rob before, a lovely fella with the head of an American Pitbull, fucking enormous great swede with this cheeky chappy face on the end of it, with the sort of expression that looks like he's about to say "pull my finger" at any given moment.

Obviously we were getting the villain rub here and the Pompey crowds were a notoriously noisy bunch of working class fuckers. Even back in the days of the FWA you were guaranteed a full house of snot nosed, Bash Street kids and mothers who looked like they earned a living pavement sweeping...with their faces.

This was no different. Out we went and it was wall to wall with people, loads standing and the first thing I noticed was people standing in the fucking aisle, which often isn't going to bode well - for them! I don't power walk to the ring like Stan Hansen swinging a cow bell, but I get a bit of a red mist on when I can see some stupid looking bastards ignorantly standing in a place I'm meant to be. It was a loud chorus of boos, which is music to your ears and always gets you right in the mood. As I was focused on my path to the ring this little leg shot out to try and trip me. I just stood there, looked down and this kid is filming with his mobile phone. I snatched it out of his hands and launched it the full length of the building, to which his father went to step forward, and then hastily backed up because I was already locked in and had sized him up for a swift upper cut.

Out came Flatliner and Frampton to a hero's reception, babies were getting thrown in the air and at last the saviours had arrived to vanquish the Viking and the mobile phone throwing angry man.

I remember Rob was quite anxious backstage and had only wrestled in a couple of matches and was unsure of how to take some of my offence, so I just told him "Don't worry mate, just go with it, you'll know how to react".

We did a test of strength which obviously he won, but I took control after cheating to get the upper hand and then sent him off for some clotheslines. If he hadn't had a lot of practice bumping then you'd never have guessed because he was horizontal in mid-air, wallop, I didn't give him any time to come to his senses and had him up again for some more shots, which he absorbed beautifully and was selling all over the place. Now after me and my tag partner had taken it in turns to beat up on Rob, I'd noticed that some props were being scattered around the ring and remembered that this had been billed as a hardcore match. I hadn't seen how these had got in here or by whom, but one of them was a fucking frying pan. So Rob tags in Flatliner who comes steaming in with his comedy routine on the Viking and turning every trick in the book until I cut him off with, guess what? the frying pan. BONK!!!! Right over his head, so hard the thing flew off its handle and into the crowd. I heard Chris say "You fucking stiff prick" as he collapsed in the corner holding his head. When he moved his hand there was a lump coming up like those Daffy Duck cartoons. Fuck me, I thought it was a prop. If you're doing a hardcore match with the Dominator and there's a frying pan lying around, you best be sure to be the first one to get hold of it because otherwise you'll have it over your head quicker than you can say "Tefal".

Anyway, the good guys came through and we were serenaded out of the arena to the same chorus of boos and fuck you's that we came in to. A wonderful evening for all the family.

I got to the back and Jonk was holding a boot up laughing his head off. "Bruv, bruv, you had one of my boots on". I thought my ankle felt dodgy, I looked down and sure enough one of the boots was almost folded over like a welly, we wore identical boots, only thing is Jonk is about three sizes up on me and we'd put each other boots on like a couple of nit wits and not noticed.

The other one that springs to mind was a show in Gosport in this tiny venue just off the Marina. We'd travelled there with Tarn and my student Dave (AWOL). It was a tag team tournament, and if I remember rightly and Jonk and I were going to absolutely savage these two lads in the opener and then go on to meet Flatliner and AWOL in the final.

We steamed through the lads in the opener in true Critical Mass style. The main event rolled round and we came bowling out of the members bar onto the dance floor. I mean, in your head it's Wembley stadium and nothing else, or why even bother getting yourself in the fucking zone, but Jonk summed it up beautifully "Let's have it right, we're coming steaming out the fucking Members bar tonight Stu" Wahahahaha! I couldn't stop laughing at how brilliantly mundane it was, we were getting changed in the bar and the ring was on the dance floor, it's as simple as that, but when the music hits and the crowd react, you could literally be anywhere, until your fucking tag partner drops that line on you like a ton of bricks and we're walking out laughing our fucking heads off.

Anyway this was the most ridiculous night of our tag career as we were there to play stooge to Flatliner. At the end of the day, his shtick isn't my thing to bounce off as The Dominator, not at all, but I know a lot of people love it and it's his hometown and we're there for him, so we did what we were getting paid to do and although it was absolute horse shit, it went down a storm. Just like the fucking air conditioning unit.

Jonk picked AWOL up for a slam and his feet went straight through the low ceiling tiles and brought a sodding air-con unit down with it. I couldn't stop fucking laughing, Jonk covered in ceiling foam and fucking debris, looking over at me with his mouth open as if I'm about to do something to help. It was just one of those nights.

We did the full comedy routine, Flatliner kissing Jonk on the lips and dancing, the 'row yer boat' spot with all four of us in a star formation and our opponents stretching us out, it was absolute fucking nonsense bell to bell, and far from a classic, but the kids and families loved seeing the big bullies get their comeuppance, so it was all good.

One of the highlights of that night for me was to see Chris backstage. He'd obviously organised for a group of young offenders to come and see the show that night with their guardians and watching him sit down with them hanging off his every word was priceless. He told them that he was glad they'd come out to see him and had a great night and not to go and be a pain in the arse to their guardians that night. It was life affirming stuff for some of those kids who looked up to Chris as I would've to a fucking Hulk Hogan or something if I was a child. They sat there starry eyed with mouths wide open like the most well-behaved kids you've ever seen when he was engaging with them. It was great stuff.

We did a show out in Sudbury somewhere for XPW before going up to Birmingham for a Sunday show for a chap called Shak Khan.

Now I'd never met Shak before but heard things about him, that he was a bit of a Walter Mitty character to say the least. His promotion was called ECW (Eastern Championship Wrestling), which was questionable to start with, and this show was being called King of the Ring with tv deals all over it and sponsors, all the bells and whistles. The roster was pretty chock full too with me and Jonk, Bulk, Crusher Curtis, Michael Kovac and many more on giant posters that read "From the village of Azad Kashmir, Pakistan for his only UK appearance.....Shak Khan"

Fuck me. Sensational stuff. He wasn't lying though, it was definitely his only UK appearance.

I can't knock him though, he met me straight away and paid us immediately before we'd even put our bags down.

Jonk and I shared a locker room with my old mate Bulk who was there with his big brother Dave who was still recovering from surgery. It was nice to see the lads again. As it was Sunday in the Asian community they had set up a sort of Indian buffet, which of course suited dear old Bulk down to the ground and he was more than happy to make use of the disabled glass lift. We'd see him coming down, really, really slowly with mitts full of samosas, poppadom's and anything else he could eat. It was all fun and games until I realised that it was him who we were on with!! I said to Jonk. "Fuck me he's going to cover us in shit out there".

Whilst getting my facepaint on I could hear "Darb, Darb!!!" Which is Bulks call to me. I went out into the lobby to find him and he was holding his sides laughing and pointing to the arena doors. I could hear this almighty noise and fuck me, they were doing prayers in the middle of the ring with the local Imam. About 50 blokes in their Sunday best all in there having a right good old pray up. The show had been delayed for an hour because of it. You couldn't write it. Well, clearly I am.

Anyway, on we went against the UK Pitbulls, comprised of Bulk and Big F'n Joe. There was fuck all people out there to witness this, probably 100 if that. Not a single woman there, all blokes between the age of 40 and 60 looking incredibly serious. I knew Bulk was in the mood for a little mischief, as is often the case, so after some superbly slow offence between the four of us, resembling a match taking place in fucking quick sand, I said to Bulk "Throw me outside". Out I went through the middle. As Jonk and Joe went about putting an end to this stinking affair, Bulk and I traded punches. I looked over his shoulder at the main section of blokes in the crowd. Now I remember distinctly Shak telling us not to fight into the crowd. So I said to Bulk "Send me in", gave him my hand and he whipped me towards the terrified Indian blokes who were all sitting together and were now scrambling to get out of the way. I turned myself upside down and crashed through about four rows of chair sending them flying like bowling pins. It was deeply satisfying and woke the buggers up. They were scrambling like fuck to get out of our way as I started throwing chairs at Bulk who was swatting them away like flies as the Indian chaps were like cats on a hot tin roof and leaping all over the place.

We met a load of them afterwards who all wanted autographs, they were all local businessmen and although they'd been pretty mute for the entire show, they absolutely loved it. Very strange occasion indeed. And guess what?? Shak won the main event against evil Austrian Michael Kovac and was carried out on the shoulders of his countrymen, quite literally, which again, was just absolutely sensational for comedy value. There wasn't a dry penis in the house.

In his mind he'd saved the world, and really who am I to argue with him. He lived his dream and we got paid, he never hurt anyone. Bulk ate about a years' worth of Indian grub as well, and it was worth going just to watch that.

Around this time I was tagging with Jonk regularly but felt I still had a good singles match in me. Even though most of my singles matches were largely short one-sided affairs, I really wanted to put right the wrong with my old mate Phil Bedwell, who was leader of the main faction The Children of Eden in EWW as Philip Bateman. The whole Eden thing was getting a lot of interest from the internet community who were seeing the polished videos we were sharing, spreading Eden everywhere like a virus.

Every single show someone new would join Eden, and as the promoter I wouldn't tell the performer who it was going to be, so when the time came it was a real shock to everyone and a real test to the acting ability of the person making the switch to see if they could work it on the fly. After all, acting is reacting, and it was always so funny watching the team genuinely looking at each other backstage wondering who would be donning the white shirt of Eden that night and turning on their family. It gave it all a very real sense of tension. And I don't give too many fucks when people say "Don't work the boys". If you want to create something different, with real palpable tension, then sometimes it's called for. If you haven't got the imagination to be able to pull the rug out from under your audience or staff then you might be in the wrong job. Keeps people on their toes you see.

Phil and I had a real five finger stinker back in about 2006 near the end of my run at The Palace in Oxford, and we went together like oil and water, it was bloody dreadful. I wanted to make up for it in a steel cage by putting him over and cementing him as a real champion to build up for a future main event with Skarlett who I was now happy with as being ready to lead EWW. There's a lot of pressure being Main Event, it doesn't matter who's show you're on or size of the crowd. The fact is, people will have paid hard earned money to see you and whether there's 100 or 1000 it really shouldn't matter, you should aim to leave it all out there and go for it, and I wasn't there anymore. Nowhere near in fact. I'd been using a lot of recreational drugs and was out of shape, looking sloppy and my head wasn't in the game at all. So I had the idea of opening the show with the big showdown in the cage, Dominator Vs Bateman, and give them one to remember this time.

The show was at Kings in Hastings, a huge venue we'd been at for the last couple of years and a wicked tech team and set up and huge cinema screen that played the live feed for the audience and our now trademarked opening mini movies.

The stage was set, and it looked like something from a Mad Max movie, all spots on the ring surrounded by the black cage and when the hundreds of people came filing in it was an awesome sight for them with all lights pointing to this fearsome structure.

Eden were by now a well-established group and the sombre piano music and the 'brown noise' siren that proceeded it always caused a hush over our big crowds. And this night was no different. There was a real electricity in the air because Phil and I were on first and the energy was really different. We'd agreed to call it out there, nothing planned, just the opening and the finish, and Phil knew that, as long as he could survive the opening three-minute flurry I'd send his way, he'd be just fine.

Phil came out alone and I came out with Titan. We started fast and I went in strong launching Phil like a rag doll from corner to corner, every time he'd try and pass me to escape I'd launch him by the throat back into the corner he came from and met him with a flurry of lefts and rights and a legit uppercut, his head was bouncing around like a ping pong ball. Meanwhile the rest of Eden appeared through the crowd and attacked Titan on the outside. Brother Drake (Liam) was climbing up the side of the cage. We were only two minutes in and it was pandemonium, the crowd were eating it up. Liam leapt from the top just as I turned round and caught him with a perfect clubbing right, WHAM!! Next, Brother Damian (Brett) was flying up the other side of the cage, I spun around, BAM!!, caught him with a spinning right and he flew out through the cage door. It was the usual three ring circus that my matches had become in the last couple of years. I'd lost a lot of my fitness, and stuff going on around me was a great way to give the illusion of action. Every time Phil would try and escape I'd cut him off. He wasn't trying to match me here, he wanted to be the coward who was trying to get the fuck away from me while his henchmen did his bidding from the sky. It was a great visual with all these bodies dressed in white flying around.

Phil cut me off and sent me headfirst into the cage a couple of times and every time he went to escape I'd stop him with a last minute grab. Now, at some point in this match I did a dropkick off the top rope, and I have no idea at which point in the match it was, or why I decided to do it, but considering I was 23 stone at this point, it wasn't too shabby. In fact I do remember Phil being a little too close to me so I didn't get as much distance, but the drop was certainly something to behold.

Phil went for his pedigree finisher which I reversed into a backdrop, tossing him over my head as I made my way to the cage door to exit and get the win. At this point Brother David shoved ref Paz out of the way, pulled the door right back and swung it shut in my face sending me back into the cage and knocking me giddy. Phil took advantage of it and left the cage, scrambling like a sewer rat out of a storm drain as I made a last grab at his boot, but to no avail.

He had got the big win as I was coming to my senses and was met by his Children of Eden all celebrating like they were kings of the world. It was a great image, their leader broken and covered in his own blood while they were parading his body in a lap of honour around the cage with me still in it. It was visually very impressive and great storytelling, and I have to say one of my very favourite matches of my career. It had the lot and got the response you dream of getting when you're a kid daydreaming about becoming a wrestler. It was everything.

To this day Phil who does film work always refers people to that match as one of his highlights as it was built on emotion and had an air of legitimacy to it that isn't often seen any more in our industry.

CHAPTER EIGHT
THE SWEET

Jonk and I were doing a few shows to get ready for the WAW TV episodes and get our Critical Mass team looking as good as possible. One of the shows was a smaller show for WAW themselves at one of their oldest venues, The Talk in Norwich, where Dave and I had been Team EWW for a year or two prior to this, and where we had had a feud with Kip Sabien and Brad Slayer.

Dave, Jonk and I drove up there that Friday night for the show, Tarn was really ill with pneumonia and couldn't work. Me and the lads stopped off near Essex somewhere for a massive KFC. More on that later....

It was our first outing with WAW for us as Critical Mass and we came in as a mystery team to answer the challenge of Sin City Killers (Ruffneck and Sam Knee) who had put out an open challenge to any team. We knew there wasn't a whole lot we could do with these two or showcase an awful lot. Ruffneck, my dear old pal Keith Colwill was always fine to work with, but Sam Knee was impossible, not a single athletic bone in his body bless him. It was as graceful a spectacle as putting the rubbish bins out.

I remember working as Death Row with Charlie Rage years before against Devils Playboys, Brett Meadows and Sam Knee. Brett was always easy and up for anything, but Sam was fucking impossible, I've never known anything quite like it, it was like having one arm and trying to stack sacks of potatoes - awkward and exhausting. I remember coming backstage after that one, which by the way was the fucking main event on that particular show, and Sweet Saraya waiting for me laughing her fucking head off, literally holding her sides saying in her raspy voice "Oh fuckin' hell babe" as I threw my shoulder pads into a corner and sat down exacerbated. To this day I've never seen her laugh as hard, she'd seen the whole ghastly affair from behind the curtain. Christ it was bad.

So when I saw our names together on the sheet I was immediately deflated, but that was the wrong emotion, because listen up kids you don't need to be match of the night to make a fucking impression, and guess what, you don't need to even be worrying about having match of the night in the first place, it's a whole show, all shapes and sizes, and there are many ways to serve up something that people will leave the venue remembering. And so I told Jonk that we had to go in hard and fast like bowling balls and smash it up, no fancy entrance, just steam in, all business, up for a fight. No quarter given and no room for complaints. If people go under, they go under, if they fight back, we'll match you toe to toe, but either way, we're going to look like massive horrible cunts while we're doing it and make it look legitimate.

That's what we did, there was none of the fancy armour and shoulder pads that we went on to wear, and we had minimalist facepaint too. We just charged in for a punch up, and to be fair, that suited the other boys well too to have it that way I think. After about six or so minutes they'd had enough and both high tailed it out of there and were counted out for their cowardice. Not exactly an emphatic conclusion but good enough that the team who offered out an open challenge were now running for the hills. We got a great response and the crowd joined in with Jonks animalistic "Oooooh Oooooh" as he did the gorilla press motion with his arms. It was hot as hell in that venue as it was a warm evening. The locker rooms were a tight squeeze so we got changed out back and had a beer outside to cool down. This Scottish kiddy called Drew was banding around these sweets that he was selling, marijuana edibles for about £5 a pop. These boiled sweets were about the size of a 10p piece and green and black.

Jonk said "Tell you what bruv, I'll treat us to some of these, I'll get one for Tarn too, it'll mellow us right out, we can have a dirty old kebab and finish the night off lovely."

The drive home was past the Thetford Forest, a long sprawling lovely track of road that on a nice evening was beautiful to drive along. One night Tarn and I saw what looked like a UFO there. No kidding. I've seen one before with one of my old students Greg Stockwell coming back from a show in Stoke on Trent, a low bright

97

white egg shape keeping up with the car and then flying over us before disappearing from sight completely. It scared the shit out of us both that night, much like this one at Thetford. A bright emerald green light illuminating the trees before slowly rising off the ground. I wanted to stop and look but Tarn insisted I keep driving. It was very unusual, but yes, we saw it whatever it was, and we often talk about it.

So this night I suggested that perhaps we stop at Thetford and go into the forest and try these sweets. But as Dave was driving we decided it may not be the best idea. We decided to get back instead. We've had some stupid ideas over the years Jonk and I, egging each other on like a couple of nit wits. Thank fuck common sense won this time. Well, almost.

So we get back to mine, Tarns on the sofa covered in a blanket, and we talk about the nights events. Jonk gets the fucking sweets out for us, and the one for Tarn. In his head he thought it would be a nice mellow end to the night as she obviously couldn't smoke a zoot with pneumonia.

There we were sucking away on these sweets. After about ten minutes I remember saying, "These are shit mate I'm not getting anything off this."

All of a sudden I remember an episode of Family Guy started and then finished in about a minute. I was like, "What the fuck was that all about?" I turned to Jonk and said "Strategy!"

He looked at me for what felt like ages and laughed his head off and said "What did you just say?"

"I don't' fucking know, what did I say?"

"You said fucking strategy bruv"

I said, "Oh fuck me I don't feel too clever here I think I'm going for a lie down." Now the rest of this story is actual witness testament from Jon Kocel himself as I don't remember much other than not being able to negotiate the corridor to the bedroom, which was now very long and uneven. I was bouncing off the walls like a human pinball.

I got into bed and felt like this was it, I can't explain the feeling of doom, but it was fucking strong. Now I was joined by Tarn who was thankfully okay, so I thought it was just me.

She got into bed and I can honestly say I've never felt anything like it. Imagine looking at your own bedroom but through a fisheye lens, it was trippy as fuck, but I knew I wasn't tripping.

Every time I closed my eyes everything would get weird, like when you've had too much to drink, but way, way worse. But it was ok as Tarn was there and she'd only had half of hers so she'd be alright to get me through this shit.

Tarn said she was going to the kitchen to get some orange juice, as vitamin c is usually a good leveller in such situations. After a couple of minutes I heard a bang, and then Tarn giggling.

I went cold and in a trepidatious way said "What's happening?" Knowing fucking damn well what was happening.

"I've forgotten how to walk" came the reply, between giggles.

I thought, "Oh fuck me no, she's gone too." So I had to get up and find my way to her up this Labyrinth style corridor which was now even longer. She was collapsed in a heap, holding the pint of orange juice valiantly in the air untroubled. I helped her to her feet, and we did the shit house shuffle back to the bedroom where I proceeded to let her go. She fell face first dead weight, cracking her head on the fireplace in our bedroom. Fuck me. She was face down, not moving. I thought she was dead. This was all too fucking much now. So I turned and shuffled as fast as I could into Jonks bedroom where he was fast asleep. He awoke to me apparently wild eyed and naked and wondered what the fuck was about to take place.

He said "Is everything ok mate?"

To which I apparently replied "No mate, it's just a bit of full on psychosis." Which does sound like the sort of stupid shit I'd say to be fair. He followed me to our room, where Tarn was thankfully on her feet rubbing her head. I helped her to the bed and climbed in. She started slapping her cheeks making popping noises with her eyes wide open as I shot the entire contents of my earlier KFC feast horizontally across the room, and it wouldn't end, it just carried on and on and on. It was a fucking horror show, Jonk was stood there horrified as I sat upright and made the feeble comment "Maybe an ambulance??"

We decided on maybe not a fucking ambulance and then I promptly shat myself and couldn't stand up at all. What sort of fuckery was going on here? Jonk had to carry me to the toilet like a fucking baby. Christ alive what a fucking sight this must've been. A few hours earlier we'd been performing in front of adoring fans and doing our thing and now I was rolling around in my own filth while my wife was playing her own face like bongos. Jonk thankfully so far was unaffected.

I sat on the shitter for what felt like five minutes but was in reality about half an hour. Some who know me would say "Twas ever thus", but on this occasion it felt like that half an hour was just endless.

Jonk carried me back to my bed (a sentence I never thought I'd have to fucking type) and then went back to his room where he promptly turned into a cricket marching on the spot and rubbing his legs together, those are his own words. He held it together to see me and Tarn alright and then after we'd eventually dropped off to sleep he was in the spare room gooning it up and down the spare room like a fucking lunatic. Christ almighty what a fucking night that was.

When I'd managed to touch down back on planet earth again that little Scottish fucker who sold Jonk these sodding things asked me how I got on with them. Well I told him exactly what happened, and dumb founded he said that fucking Xpac Sean Waltman, had about ten of the fucking things. He must have some next level kind of receptors that geezer that's for fucking sure. What was intended to be a chilled-out evening of chat and sliding into a nice melting sleep was all of us turning into the cast of One Flew Over the Cuckoo's Nest - and very nearly a real-life game of Cluedo. Miss Skarlett in the bedroom, with the fireplace. Ma'lud.

Who'd have ever believed me and Jonks story? We'd have been sent down for that for sure.

We were well tuned up now as Critical Mass and done a number of gigs together beaning people off in quick fashion, but up until now, hadn't been tested. It was time for the trip up to Norwich again for their first foray into television land with a bunch of long nights at Epic studios which were always a lot of fun, but boy were they long. Cut up into hour long episodes for TV they'd run matinee shows and evening shows and get a good eight hours of television in one day.

The rosters were fucking enormous and the first one featured WWE starts including Hall of Famer, Scott Hall who they brought in as the Commissioner, Lisa Marie and Ken Anderson.

Jonk and I were once again on with the Sin City Killers, dear old Keith Colwill and Sam Knee.

Nobody wants to see they're going on with me and Jonk because they know they're not going to get much, but by the same fucking token, Sam Knee was the last person we wanted to be showcasing with. It was like pissing up a rope, fun for nobody. But hey, we'd make it work.

It was no bother either as we were all assigned agents for our matches, most of whom were a handpicked selection of legendary ex professionals from the World of Sport era such as Frank 'Chic' Cullen and Johnny Kincaid. Of course, the time schedules were tight as a nuns fanny so there was no wiggle room to fuck around, and of course those times included entrances. I think our match was something like six minutes, which to me and Jonk was a blessed relief, because what could go wrong in that time?

Keith had a bit of a wobble before we went out, it was all a bit much for him I think and he felt a lot of pressure because at the time this was all quite a big deal, and a lot of money had been spent on getting this right. In fact, as the months went on and we kept going back to record more tapings, the look of the shows got better and better to the point where they were easily on a par with anything across the pond. The whole set up was one of the best I've seen in this country.

Anyway, we dominated the match, the highlight being both Keith and Sam spilling to the outside as I pulled the rope down and Jonk flew over the top with all the grace of a deckchair onto the pair of them. Nobody saw that coming, the huge motherfucker flying over the top, The problem was he nearly KO'd poor Keith with his bollocks in the process. He felt them separate over Keiths forehead like a knotted hankie and Christ didn't we hear about it all night. Keith holding his head and Jonk holding his swollen genitals. We kept it simple with a DDT and splash combo, but people seemed to like us, and nobody got killed, so it was a decent job.

I can't remember entirely if it was this taping or one later on, but I remember I had a falling out with Scott Hall. Now bear in mind, he was one of the greatest performers in the world in the early to mid-nineties and certainly one of the best big men of all time, along with having one of the greatest wrestling minds. But on this occasion, fuck all of that, he pissed me off.

He'd taken exception to my chops, the overhand one, which I love because it goes off like a firecracker because of the speed of my wrist. But Scott, who was a big fan of me and Jonks look, said he loved my punches, and he was a man who threw one of the best working punches of all, so that was nice for a small thing, but the overhand chop, to him it looked too much like a "sissy slap". Jonk went quiet and looked at me for a second before I looked Scott straight in the eye and said, "Well do you fucking fancy one then?"

To which he replied "Come again?"

"You fucking heard." To which he turned on his heel and walked out the door.

"Cunt" I think is also something I might have said....

Ah well, it wasn't long before Scott and I were at the bar having a drink. He was fascinated by our little group, Team EWW, comprised of myself, Jonk, Tarn and Dave. He ended up asking to be the agent for our matches in future as he felt we could do so much more, and spending time with him really ended up being a very enriching experience. There was a man who'd been one of the biggest names in the business and conquered his own addictions, but still had a childlike gleam in his eye for the world of wrestling and just wanted the best for people still in it.

Jonk was sinking a bottle of whiskey afterwards to numb the pain of his goolies and I was just fed up, the match was clunky but thankfully very short, nobody needed to see us four arseholes in the ring lumbering around for twenty minutes, so it was short and hard. Which is also the title of my sex tape.

Anyway, we went off to a big pub that night, as it was a celebration of sorts. A big day for WAW as they'd secured some big names for the whole next year's tapings and had a really solid backer in Amit Medina and everyone was happy. The Knights, who were always well known for their hospitality, had hired a big bar for the night and laid on a load of grub for the wrestlers.

I'd managed to borrow a big old Mercedes people carrier from work and we ended up having Mr Anderson, Scott Hall and Lisa Marie all squashed into the van to get to this pub along with my lot and Dave driving. Jonk who was well and truly inebriated by this point insisted on showing Lisa Marie his injured bollocks in the van. They looked all shiny and polished, not worn and weathered like mine. Hairless new pink things they were.

I ended up drinking a skin full and playing 'Gay chicken' with Scott Hall, which I fucking won by the way. I could feel his whiskers rasping against my beard and smell the booze on his breath. We backed off as if we'd both pissed on an electric fence. Which I have for the record and wouldn't recommend it. But yeah, you can keep your Intercontinental title at Wrestlemania Ten mate, I just spanked you at Gay chicken at the Dog and Duck in Norwich!

We took them back to the hotel which we were all booked into after bundling Scott into the back of our people carrier with him in his old Southern drawl going "Fuuuck bro, fuuuuuck".

Someone was trying to give Dave the directions to the hotel near the airport and Scott was saying "Does this cab driver even fucking know where he's going bro?" Poor old Dave.

By the time we got back to the hotel he was so bamboozled by the nights shenanigans that he leant forward with a fist full of money "Give this to the cab driver bro". After explaining for the third time he was actually with us, and had literally just been in the same bar with us, he finally got it.

We gathered in the hotel and were all pretty post show happy, someone gave us a little bag of weed, I had some fags (cigarettes for the American readers, I don't want to get cancelled again) but no Rizla. So Jonk came up with the genius idea of skinning up with the Old Testament from the Gideons bible dutifully kept in all chain

103

hotel drawers. I always wondered why they were there as I blew out that beautiful smoke. Ahh yes!

The next tag team match we had there was a triple tag team match with us against The Essex Boys and guess what, Sam Knee and Keith again. I really must've done something awful in a previous life for this lark.

Jonk took most of the white meat baby face heat which was daft as the bugger was the biggest in the ring, and in fact the largest on the entire bloody show. He sold from pillar to post. It was too much, I told Jonk before to stop over selling, but this angered Scott Hall who was watching on monitor. He said exactly that when we went backstage and used the immortal line in his famous Razor Ramon style drawl "Bro, selling for the jabronis like that, you went from stud to dud". Poor old Jonk looked mortified, Scott was one of his wrestling heroes and he didn't want to let anyone down. But as it goes it was fucking good advice from one of the greatest workers who's ever lived, so you don't get things like that too often.

He tagged me in and I did the old house of fire deal with Paul Tyrell and Phil Powers. I sent Powers off for a backdrop and sent him up high even though it felt like he really didn't fancy it, he was usually quick at getting up but on this occasion looked lethargic as he got to his feet and I clobbered him with two clotheslines.

The finish came and once again was a clunky old affair, I was up on the middle rope, Jonk whipped Sam Knee in and I came off with a clothesline and pinned Sam, who just could never take a fucking bump no matter how hard you hit him. He'd go down forwards or sideways or on his arse. I did fucking level him in the hope he'd take a half decent bump, but no, instead he flopped onto the floor like a dropped lasagne and was crying that I'd broken his nose. I hadn't for the record.

The following morning when I woke up my phone was lit up with several messages and voicemails from delighted wrestlers who were thanking me for my work. I had no idea what they were talking about until I found out that Phil Powers was in hospital after our match and had told everyone that I'd fucked him up, and he'd even put pictures of himself up on social media from hospital. If I wanted to 'fuck him up' I'd have tucked the little cunt up better than that that's for sure, he's always been a dirt bag, a liar and a bully, but on this occasion I was working and being professional on my friends show. That wasn't the time or the place, and in fact I'd worked with him at least three other times up to that point and on those occasions he was relieved after and had thanked me, so why he went off running to the few cronies left who actually talked to him and having a cry up I have no idea.

At this point I'd been outing a few promoters and wrestlers alike, who were known abusers and groomers, on my podcast Stiff Right Hand. I forget how it all started, but before long both Tarnya and I were getting inundated with screenshots and messages from youngsters in the business who had proof that they'd been getting inappropriate pictures sent to them along with grooming that was going on across the board. "Take pictures for me and I'll put you on the show" and that sort of thing. One promoter from the Midlands was sending messages of a sexual nature to a young female trainee who contacted me, she was just 14. The conversation was suggestive and then became coercive and eventually of course he couldn't help but expose himself in the messages to this girl, despite her on two occasions clearly stating her age. He's not promoting anywhere anymore, and his wife was none too thrilled with his insistence on sending pictures of his silly looking genitalia.

The patterns were so alarmingly similar in almost every occasion and over a couple of years it was so prevalent that we had a hot desk set up with Hastings Police to deal with it, but the problem was that on most occasions the victims were too scared to talk to the police, they were happy to have a safe intermediary like myself or Tarn to go to, but the police seemed to be a bridge too far for some despite having some very concrete proof.

I was asked to do podcasts about the subject and there were a couple of people on Twitter, where it's the norm to be faceless, who were jumping on the bandwagon and putting out aggressive tweets calling out some of these wrestlers and promoters and encouraging social media pile-ons. Which wasn't helpful to the cause. This of course then went on to give credence to the "Innocent until proven guilty" brigade who were more often than not fans of the certain wrestlers under the microscope and taking the fight to the accusers or occasionally me, as if the whole thing was created to ruin a career.

Usually the basement dwelling neck bearded keyboard warrior style wrestling nerd would come out with utter gems such as "Well (name) was nothing but nice to me", and then be absolutely gobsmacked as to why the victim may have been hesitant to report it via the correct channels. The burden of proof once again expected of every victim to endure more humiliation or tests just to prove that the thing which left them destroyed in the first place actually occurred. It's wrong. Absolutely fucking wrong, and the wrestling world was one of the worst breeding grounds for it. Every time one door shut, another one opened. I remember one evening Tarn and I sat across the kitchen table from one another, both on different calls to two different victims of two different people. We were finishing up at work and then taking this on in the evenings, it was wearing, but fucking necessary. I remember sitting opposite her and her head was in her hands, she was exhausted, it was impossible not to be.

The campaign made its way across the pond and promoters and wrestlers were getting outed and cancelled, some top name abusers were getting removed from rosters and television and as usual the fanbases of some of the individuals, largely thirty something white males, were all glassy eyed and full of spite that people were "out to get" their heroes. Just like over here, loyal fan bases of disgruntled man-children were growing ready to hurl their toys if their favourite was about to get named.

I was accused of all sorts from some of these daft idiots who literally only exist in this subculture, the normal wrestling fan nowadays are so ingrained in wrestling thanks to the knowing the ins and outs of a ducks arsehole, thanks to the internet, feel that they are as much a part of the industry as the wrestlers they pay to see. They were on Twitter in droves upset and having a right old cry up if their favourite was removed from a show due to an ongoing investigation. I was called a Nazi due to my profile stating that I was born in Hamburg and told to go back to my own fucking country by the same genius who was angry at my online interventions and podcasts! Wahahahaha, I spat my tea across the room when I read that.

Some old pig who was a big fan of Pip 'Bubblegum' Cartner was so incensed about the claims that he was abusive to his then girlfriend that she claimed in a Twitter thread that I was earning money from it and pocketing bribe money to keep quiet about certain people whilst slaughtering others, like it was some kind of verbal protection racket!

I made the mistake of answering some of these idiots who were sliding into my DM's and that was my first mistake. Much like choosing to step in a dog turd rather than over it, there is no good outcome. Expecting someone to think rationally when they are supporting a potential abuser, accused groomer or paedophile.

One of the things that angered me most during this time though was some people in the industry's flippant attitude to it, with some saying "You could ruin the business for everyone mate and it's going really well at the moment." Basically - don't spoil our beloved wrestling!!!!

Now I'm going to do the bloke a favour by not naming him because he's a friend of mine and I've wrestled for him too, however I was so fucking angered by this selfish and short sighted attitude that I didn't wrestle for him again. People had turned a blind eye to abusers in wrestling for years, and often the ones who had an eye for the young boys or girls were just figures of fun. And it's all very well saying "Well times were different", but my coach Adrian Street famously battered Jimmy Savile back in the late 60's when it was bandied around the dressing room, as what would be seen today no doubt as "a bit of banter", that Savile would brag about lines of underage girls waiting for him outside his dressing rooms and that he'd pick who he wanted.

Adrian tore a chunk out of his scalp and he never returned to wrestling again. Yet here we were in around 2015 and some so-called veterans were telling me "You'll never win, we've been trying for years", and then what, just gave up presumably yeah?

I had a promoter from London tell me that he was going "Straight to the police station" because we'd been sent evidence of him telling a young trainee to strip naked in the ring van amongst other things. I let him know that his name was all over Twitter and so panicked was he as I let him know that I'd seen the evidence, that I received a panicked phone call within seconds of the message dropping with him shrieking hysterically down the phone and getting an octave higher each second. It was pure panic. Sounds guilty right?

So these fuckers are well and truly out there crawling around on the petri dish of life and all it took was someone to peer down the microscope to unsettle them, and make them realise that there were still people out there who care enough about what they're doing to say "we know what you're fucking up to". Some have been cancelled, some are on registers and some are still, after all this time, unbelievably trying to weasel back into the wrestling world under different names so desperate are they to be involved. And of course, there are the promoters who turn a blind eye completely and let the guilty continue to perform on their shows because "They've always been nice to me."

But as long as I've still got a breath in my body I will continue to make life very difficult and uncomfortable for these parasites. It just baffles me that some people with children of their own don't think it's as important a mission to make as I have done in the past. Wonders will never cease.

We were up and down doing shows for the Knights at Epic and working in Europe too around this time, doing France and Belgium. In WAW we were constantly doing six-man tags with me, Jonk and Dave beating people left and right as Team EWW. We'd had some custom music made by Len Davies who'd got Tony Iommi from Black Sabbath to record a wicked instrumental for us exclusively for the tv show, it was a banger too.

The arena set up was improved every time we went up there, they were constantly adding to it or changing it and it was a really impressive looking set. Whether it was against veteran workers such as Jynx, Robin Lekime or Ken Anderson or taking on the youngsters, we faced a shed load. And for the most part it included Jonk or I losing our shit and belting people with our helmets. Perhaps I should rephrase that.

We were knocking people bandy with our entrance armour. I wouldn't want you to get the wrong idea.

One that stood out was a six man against some WAW youngsters, one of whom was a lad called Sonny Smasher. He was a nice kid and very enthusiastic. As per the brief, we beat them from pillar to post. Afterwards we went down to the car park area for a cheeky cigarette and there was Zak Knight giving young Sonny a right old bollocking. Sonny had apparently got upset with our style, hadn't realised the rather obvious size difference and said we'd "taken liberties", and upon seeing Jonk and I coming down the stairs he ran like a shit house rat out of a storm drain off into the night in his fringed wrestling tights, with Zak in hot pursuit up the street. Fuck me It was funny.

The kid came back (with his mum to boot!) and explained he didn't really know what the taking of liberties meant, and that he'd never been hit so hard in his life and didn't know what to do. He didn't have a mark on him. I calmly explained to the poor kid that if Jonk and I wanted to take liberties with someone that they would be in far worse condition than he currently was, and

certainly not in any fit state to do a Usain Bolt up Norwich city centre.

We always had good times up there no matter who they put us on with. My old pal from Germany Demolition Davies was always fun. He's a lovely fella and for a man of his size moves with superb agility. Jonk and I tagged against him and some Scandinavian lanky fella who wasn't really up to it. Of course, Davies bumped himself around like a rubber ball and made everything look great, but Jonk ended up getting whiplash off this thin streak and got a right old stinger.

Then as we came through the curtain one of the production team told him to watch where he was walking because of some cables they were laying down, but she did it in an unwise manner and hadn't quite read the fucking room "Dude, watch where you're going".

As she said it, I was behind him and immediately put my hands on his back to keep him walking. "Watch where you're going you fucking cheeky cunt!! Why don't you watch where you're fucking going?!?!" He went fucking mental, when he does that he grows in size and becomes like the abominable snowman, but his face elongated like the painting 'The Scream'. Fucking punching walls and going absolutely insane. Just what we needed in our tiny dressing room me and my team, Jonk in a fucking flare up swinging his arms around. Tarn, as usual in these situations, was great at calming the situation down with common sense and a tall glass of shut the fuck up.

He'd expended so much energy on this jumped-up little production intern that he'd forgotten entirely about his stinger and was now in the throes of concussion, sweating and dry heaving.

He insisted on going down to the basement car park for a cigarette at which point he collapsed and the paramedics at Epic were very good with him. Jack Swagger was walking past and said "Why's he down there"

"He got bored mate, nothing to see here"

"Ah okay cool" he replied going about his business the big daft looking sod. Fuck me. Oxygen must be in short supply on the top floor when you're that tall.

A team of paramedics arrived with all the kit and one of them asked Jonk if he was bothered by needles. Oh how we laughed!

CHAPTER NINE
THE SHOW MUST GO ON

Jonk went through a phase of a lot of wrestling injuries over a short period of time, ranging from the sublime to the ridiculous. I think it was around 2015 to 2017, and we were in a tag team tournament and about to become the first ever tag team champions in EWW. The semi-final we wiped out a team to get into the final and the team of Blitzkrieg and Deadly Nightshade, who were two of my students, stormed the ring and took us out. Jonk was facing the crowd and Nightshade came in with a low blow to take his leg out from under him. Jonk has these ruddy great plates of meat and naturally stands at 9:15, and of course, his ankle went. Not just rolled - but went. The action replay on it was fucking horrendous, the big black wrestling boot folded over like a loose welly, it was enough to make your arsehole pucker up. This very well nearly fucked the night up entirely as we were in the main event for the belts, but we taped his ankle up with electrical tape, as is the wrestling way, squeezed his boot on and he did a whole 15 minute match on it.

He went up to the hospital, luckily our venue that night was opposite the Conquest hospital in Hastings, but being a Saturday night he was up there a while. Once again Tarn was luckily on hand as a porter set him off by saying something and crutches went flying through the air in A&E and the door smashed open, with Tarn telling him to fucking behave himself.

The worst of all was a match against two more of my trainees Lupo Lee and Grayson Dawn, two of the nicest kids I've ever taught. Neither of them have a bad bone in their body and you couldn't wish to meet two harder working humble lads. They're both a credit to me and our Academy.

Anyway, this night I was keen for Jonk to call the match as he was used to just getting in there and doing what I told him, which was great, but I wanted him to start learning the art of constructing a match.

112

So there we were the four of us, in the ring. The giants of EWW Critical Mass vs the nervous and green as goose shit hometown kids, Grayson and Lupo. Blue eyes vs blue

eyes. The crowd were split down the middle but there was a crackle of electricity in the air, an almost pensive feel from people who knew they were about to see the lions eat the acrobats. They were indeed about to see someone badly hurt, but not what any of us were expecting. It was the Sussex Coast College which was our biggest venue, and it was absolutely packed out that night.

The thing about Pro wrestling that galls me is, and I'm sure I'll have mentioned this before, but dealing with the amount of people who don't give it the credit it deserves and write it off as fake. You wouldn't sit at Cineworld and write the action off on screen as fake, and we only get one take, and one angle, oh, and I nearly forgot, it's full contact! When you put all that together, you can understand why a decent wrestling school is crucial. However, due to the nature of what we do, sometimes things can go wrong, that's the nature of the job. And on this occasion, all the cards were stacked in exactly the correct order for disaster to strike.

Jonk was locking up with Grayson to start out, they'd literally been in the ring no longer than two minutes and the idea was for Grayson to rile the big man with a slap to the face. Nothing more than that. He slaps Jonk and the crowd did the "Oooooh" as they knew they were about to see a hiding. I was on the tag rope and Jonk checked his mouth with his hand and I thought nothing of it. The next minute he was circling to the other side of the ring and I noticed a steady stream of claret running down his huge chest. His mouth was frothing with blood and we'd barely even started. His eyes were nervously darting over to me and I knew something was badly wrong. He went through the motions and tagged me, and as he came over he said something but I couldn't hear it, it was muffled, "Bruv I'm fucked' I think he said. I could see that much. So Grayson and I finished the match and we ended up shaving about five minutes off it as I knew Jonk was going to need swift medical attention as he was fading in and out on the tag rope and we still had another team to run in on us yet and beat us down again until we bled. Well, Jonk was already ahead of the game on that front, but he did it and finished the job and I helped him to the back. It transpired that his jaw was completely separated, it was a right mess, the whole bottom row of teeth weren't where they should've been and I've never seen anything like it. He must've been in fucking agony.

The slap must've been at entirely the wrong angle on the wrong part of the jaw, I've watched it back and it was the most innocuous looking slap too, they couldn't have replicated that result if they'd done it 100 times over. But of course, on the live show, tits up we go once again. But to his credit, old Jonk had a bunch of very nasty injuries but he still got the job done. He'd go several shades of mental afterwards I grant you, but in front of the crowd, nobody would've known.

He ended up in the Conquest yet again before being moved to Brighton where he had to have a steel plate put in his face, the poor sod. He was on chicken noodle soup all day every day. He said he never wants to see another bowl of fucking chicken noodle soup as long as he lives. Monday "Chicken noodle soup", Tuesday "Chicken noodle soup" etc etc.

Dear old Grayson Dawn is a young lad with a bright future and a great attitude, I dearly hope all of my students make it of course, but Kiernan (his real name) has it all and if he is persistent, which unless you are incredibly fortunate is something you need to be, I have no doubt will be a big star one day.

I felt sorry for him on the night this happened, he was absolutely shellshocked, the colour drained out of him and he was staring at the floor in disbelief. I remember Darren Walsh saying "Fuck me, he's got a career in Boxing with a right hand like that he's better than George Foreman".

In fact it was an eventful night all in all as I ended up knocking out some absolute fucking moron in a nightclub later that night. A nightclub who were our sponsors for that event unfortunately. But this arsehole had purposely shoved Tarn as she was helping a very inebriated friend off of the dance floor, and had not seen me following closely behind.

He turned, sweaty stupid face contorted in drunken anger and walked beautifully onto a straight left that according to reports from bystanders saw him skid ten feet on his back on the dance floor. And I never use my left.

Just for the record to any potential sponsors I don't usually make a habit of laying out punters at your establishments, but this was a fucking bad move on his part, he was a lairy prick and I was in a bad mood, and that spelt lights out for the scrote.

Jonk was out of action for some time and unable to work the doors which he always loved to do. Loves a bit of the old door does old Jonk. Beating people to a cream for a wage, fucking loved it he did. He hates booze hounds as much as I do. I absolutely detest pub culture to the point it makes me feel violent, and I don't mind admitting it. I recently went for a few days getaway to Warwickshire to see my old friend Ginny and whilst stopping en-route to catch up with some old school chums I hadn't seen in nearly thirty years, I stopped at a pub at the bottom of Burford high street called the Cotswold Arms for a bit of lunch. Watching the world go by in a sleepy little Hamlet, height of summer. Fucking glorious. Only to have the peace ruined by some daft, braying Scaffolder arseholes who'd knocked off early. Booze and sun do not mix, and this establishment in my opinion was well out of their league for starters. In no uncertain terms I told them to shut the fuck up or I'd be out of my box, and that they wouldn't want to see me when I'm hungry, or something along those lines.

To be fair, they were compliant in shutting the fuck up, probably thinking I was some eccentric grey haired old lunatic, and they'd have been right. But there's a reason I've made it to 47 with these good looks still intact lads. So keep the fucking noise down.

If you read my first book (and if you haven't I have to question why you've decided to fucking well start here) you'll know that I spent many years doing doors in Oxford and seeing girls coming in looking a million dollars, and then leave covered in their own sick and having pissed themselves. It makes you realise we have got more problems with alcohol in this country than literally anything else. I used to love a beer, especially after a wrestling show, sinking a few cold ones was always like the best medicine. Now I can't think of anything worse.

But yeah, poor old Jonk, he'd had some fucking bad luck in his short career. One of the legitimately toughest young men I've ever known, he's sprayed walls with people's grey matter and teeth all over Crawley and most men would think twice about crossing him regardless of status, yet the phoney old wrestling business had been responsible for some of the most physically painful episodes in his life, and they have the nerve to call us actors. The nurses from the Conquest by now were on first name terms with him and he might as well have had his own bed in the corner.

We were straight back to tagging when his face had healed up. He had a slightly gaunter look in the face but was as gigantic as ever. We did some shows for Brett Meadows World War Wrestling up in Suffolk in a freezing cold showground. Always really good shows with Brett, he gave everything to his products, but fuck me was that venue bloody cold!

I remember it well, it was a massive tent with the wind whipping in one end and out the other like a tunnel, it was fucking brutal, and I rarely feel the cold. The changing rooms were hastily put together separated off areas with ply and it looked like the set of Takeshi's Castle (so I'm told). I remember one of them Tarn huddling in the corner wrapped up like a mad grandma all hunched and angrily nursing a flask of coffee she'd rather cleverly thought to bring.

Being wrestlers obviously we're required to be in various forms of undress and my nipples were out and my penis was firmly inside my body It was a real biting cold and I was about to go on with this lad who's name I forget, but he was a villain and had chosen a really fucking lousy time to cut the longest promo known to man. He thought he was getting some tasty heat from the crowd, but in reality he was getting "Shut the fuck up" heat - the only heat in that place as it goes. I was doing some Hindu squats in front of a huge gas heater to try and stay warm, and every time I was ready for my music to hit, he'd start talking again and I could feel icicles on the end of my nose. Three minutes in and I was starting to get a little thin lipped,

116

which delighted Brett who used to take great pleasure in watching me get pissed off. Finally my music came on and I wasted no time in getting in the ring and belting the bloke straight in the chops. Have that you fucker.

I remember up in Norwich for WAW again and Tarn by now was the longest reigning British champion in Bellatrix history and was laying waste to all comers. The rest of us lumps were Team EWW and had just about every style of tag match you could imagine. Out of all those we did for the TV tapings, one of the funniest of all was a 'sin bin' match where you'd get carded by the ref for a misdemeanour like in football and sent to the sin bin like in ice hockey. One teams group of chairs was one side of the entrance ramp and the others on the other. Once again I have to apologise for my lousy memory here as I can't remember our opponents, but what a stupendous cluster fuck this was. The referee old Dave Finch was so carried away with dishing out cards that at one stage nearly all of us were sat in the sin bin scratching our bollocks leaving one bloke in the ring. Don't think that match made it to air.

The WAW were upping the ante each time with these and bringing in bigger stars each time like Rey Mysterio, Ted DiBiase, Mickie James and the legendary Madusa. So-Cal Val, was there, but what a tedious piece of work she was, looked like someone had fired a paint ball gun full of make up at a Cabbage Patch doll.

One of my favourites was Jesus Rodriguez, the former valet to legendary piece of shit Alberto Del Rio. Jesus was a very decent worker and was often used in WWE to work with the new guys at try -outs, not only that but he was the foil for Del Rio's South American aristocrat character and some would say the more entertaining of the two.

I remember us piling out of our people carrier eager for mischief. One of those days when something was in the air. We arrived in the middle of a meet and greet, of which we were meant to be a part of, and luckily someone had saved us a table so we quickly piled all of our merch out and got to shaking hands and signing bits.

117

Over the years working for WAW we've made many good friends up there out of the legions of loyal WAW fans, and so our table kept piling up with beers as people were pleased to see us. I was pleased to see the beers and Jonk and I were guzzling them down quick time and it wasn't even lunch time yet. Terry Gauci was the talented WAW Master of Ceremonies, a really lovely fella Terry, like an old school song and dance all-rounder he was, smart and always charming to talk to. Anyway he was going around with the microphone chatting to some of the punters and wrestlers alike. By the time he got to our table I could see him nervously make his way over to me, he knew that I had a gleam in my eye at this point and wanted that fucking microphone. I'm pretty sure I heard the wife say, "Oh don't give him the mic for fucks sake", as she gets to hear my bullshit without the benefit of a PA system on a daily basis.

Anyway, by this point I was fairly well oiled and so took the mic and proceeded to take aim at poor old Jesus whom I hadn't actually even met yet. The poor geezer was minding his own business talking to female fans when I clocked it and said something along the lines of "Oi Rodriguez, I see you over there chatting our birds up, I know your game sunshine.....Oi love, don't buy his 8x10's!" it was something like that or equally inappropriate, there was laughter everywhere and he was doing his very best to remain charming, although had a wonderful rosy shade to his cheeks. By the time Terry came back around he'd been asked categorically not to let me have the microphone, Christ it was funny. Jesus came over and we chatted and I made him walk around the venue holding my hand. I have no idea why I do these things. But he was a great sport and a lovely soul. Indeed it's true to say that Jesus loves me.

It was a great venue that Epic studio in Norwich. One of the weirdest things happened to me there. I often get asked what's the strangest thing that's ever happened to me in wrestling, and I have to say, one of the very strangest happened to me there in Epic Studios, and in the toilets no less. It's always a bit risky when the performers have to share the same toilets as the fans, and during one of the Bellatrix shows I nipped into a cubicle for a post Subway poo. Mid turd, this hand appeared under the cubicle with a bit of paper and a pen and a man's voice said "Dominator can I have your autograph please?"

Fuck me, I was curling one out and you know when you get to the point of no return and getting your normal speaking voice out is a bit challenging? I said "Who shall I sign it too for fucks sake?" to which he replied, "Can you just say best wishes." Honestly, pick your moments people!

I remember Flatliner drawing on faces of kids, thrilled to be daubed on by the big man. Their parents not so thrilled as he'd done moustaches and glasses on some, but in permanent marker. It was like gangs of miniature Groucho Marx's running around after shows and it was a case of "Fuck me, who's given Chris the permanent marker pens?"

And up in Halifax on the FWA Evil Intentions show with the 7-foot Jawz who was so intent on giving his autographs that even when this little girls ink ran out in her pen, so determined was he to sign her arm he basically carved JAWZ into her arm with the dry nip. She's probably in her 30's with that to this day. She was really happy with it too. They make 'em different up north.

They say that the most stressful times in your life are moving house, changing job and having children. Well, I'd like to add retiring from a 25-year wrestling career to that list.

It was a tumultuous build up to my final event after coming to the decision to retire. I knew it was coming, I had been struggling with tremendous ankle pain from a badly pinned foot surgery after a bad car crash many years ago, and some days the pain even lying down was unbearable. To this day my right foot is off set at a peculiar angle to my ankle and I roll over on it badly. That coupled with being 23 stone is a pretty perfect storm for some serious pain.

I enjoyed teaching my wonderful students, they provided me with a huge amount of pride and laughter in equal measure and that was the main part of the wrestling business that I was very keen to remain in my life. My Extreme Academy of Wrestling was one of the greatest schools in the country and we'd been the first to design a thorough safeguarding programme alongside trained and certified officers who worked with us on this, which was for all of our male and female students to protect them from the ever-increasing threat of being groomed or abused in the wrestling business.

Of course, when we began the Speaking Out movement in the British wrestling scene as I mentioned earlier, we were accused of "Spoiling the job for people" and told, "It's always been like that". So when we launched our huge protection scheme and online version for others to follow, there was a tsunami of people who copied us, unashamedly within days, some of whom without any irony at all having been working with a number of the accused to begin with and, with very watered down versions of ours, hurriedly trying to mimic our safe family ethos.

For the most part it was a smoke screen from playtime promoters who got their jollies off controlling young men and women.

Funnily, but unsurprisingly enough, some of the first to be speaking from the roof tops were several shady promoters from all female shows who thought they were male bastions of the female voice, when in actual fact they were just hastily papering over the cracks before anyone looked too closely at them. That along with Promotions who harboured and defended abusers, giving them regular work and spending a lot of time gaslighting victims along with a slew of basement dwelling pasty virgin boys who hated seeing their favourites getting outed. It truly showed the UK business in the worst light, and Tarnya and I were sometimes vilified by people for spoiling everyone's fun. Can you fucking believe it?

People's lives were getting smashed apart by little twerps who were milk monitors dressed up as wrestlers, and we were getting brave fuckers typing no end of shit about us online because it hurt their feelings. It went on for a long, long time and involved hours of telephone time.

Our Safeguarding officers and policy were airtight and the video that we put out alongside it to explain all bullet points was something we were incredibly proud of. But whilst all the other promotions were busy patting themselves on the back even though all the leg work with qualified counsellors and specialists had all been put in place by us two years previously without fanfare, we just carried on doing our job and went on to introduce several other new requirements into our Academies structure too, along with talks on how to conduct yourself on social media.

The older I got the less I wanted to socialise as my mental health was very slowly on the wane, and I was very aware of it. Old habits were creeping back in like unwanted repetitive thoughts which I was constantly internally rewarding myself with, it could become crippling and interfere with my daily life, cause me to be late to appointments or even worse, get stuck in my own obsessive world.

For the last couple of years I'd been doing shows for other promoters but not really wanting to perform, I didn't want to be around people from the fans to the locker rooms, I felt caged and I hated it, this wasn't why I got into the wrestling business. What the fuck was I doing? If I wasn't giving value for money to the paying public, I needed to get the fuck out of it. People can sniff if you're not in the game, they're not stupid.

So I made the decision and sat down with Tarnya. She was surprised but very supportive. I then announced it to all of my students at the Academy, some of whom were tearful which broke my heart a bit if I'm honest. I then put it on my social media pages and some of the response from around the world was quite staggering, ranging from sadness to thank fuck for that.

One of the nicest I remember was from the remarkable Justin Richards, a wonderful man, wrestler and teacher who said that I was one of the very few wrestlers in Europe who gave an air of terrifying legitimacy in everything I ever did in the ring. That was all I'd ever wanted, to be real and make people believe, as all my heroes did when I used to watch, some made me believe for a lot longer than others could, and those were my heroes. The ones who made me believe. So to me, that was the highest compliment I could get.

My original Coach Adrian Street contacted me along with Miss Linda and said how proud they both were of me, which again, meant a huge deal.

In the coming months I came away from wrestling completely because I wanted my final match to be a spectacle, and I was asked to do one last match for several promotions in the run up to it, but I didn't want it to dilute the response to my own show, and thus declined.

I was contacted by Lee Canderton, who was also known back in the day as Lee Bamber, a very well-known old school referee and Master of Ceremonies. He told me that I was to be honoured with a Lifetime Achievement Award at the prestigious British Wrestlers Reunion in Kent in early September a month before the big show. He asked if I would accept the award, of course it was an honour to be given an award that had in the past gone to the likes of Johnny Saint, Mark Rocco and many others who I grew up idolising every Saturday afternoon, I was taken aback to say the least.

I took a few people up there with me on the day. It was held as ever as Wayne Bridges' famous pub, the aptly named 'The Bridges' in Kent, a beautiful old pub underneath a huge railway arch just outside of Dartford.

It was a blisteringly hot Sunday afternoon and we were greeted by some familiar faces straight away. The flamboyant Johnny Kincaid was there with his huge ear to ear grin and met me with a solid handshake. A wonderful man is Johnny. He always has wonderful stories to tell and I could listen to him for hours. He's also a fantastic poet and would regale you at the drop of a hat with one of his poems in between telling a story. A skilled and charming raconteur with a gleam in his eye.

I heard the raspy Scottish voice of Frank 'Chic' Cullen call my name and sure enough there he was sat on one of the benches, beer in hand and a grin on his face.

Chic was up there as one of my very favourites as a child, he could do it all. He trained with the Hart family in Stampede, and along with Dynamite Kid and Chris Benoit was a gifted aerialist who was years ahead of his time. When he came back to England and was on World of Sport his matches stood out from the others by a mile. Deft flips and springs, nip ups and missile dropkicks, I'd never seen anything like it amongst the largely mat based gentlemanly combat you'd see on the television. With his blonde mullet he looked like a rock star flying through the air.

He was one of our agents at WAW on numerous occasion he'd be assigned to us and was so easy to work with. I loved seeing him, another cheeky faced veteran who could make you laugh at the drop of a hat.

As we walked in we met the Legendary stuntman Eddie Kidd OBE who was also being given an award on the same day. Eddie was the UK equivalent of Evel Knievel but he was sadly paralysed following brain damage after performing a stunt at the Bulldog Bash event, which finished his remarkable career. I'd seen loads of his incredible death-defying stunts when I was a child including the most famous where he jumped the Great Wall of China in 1993. If you haven't seen it, get on Google, it's quite something.

Like I said it was a gloriously hot day and the beer garden at the Bridges was absolutely heaving with people, you couldn't see a blade of grass. My old friend Chris 'Flatliner' Manns was there with his trademark chunky jewellery and tiger print top stretched across his enormous frame. One day I hope he finds a place that sells his size in clothes.

The awards ceremony started, and I was already three pints in. People were buying me drinks left and right and I had a line of them there for me. Now the problem is, I have always had a peculiar relationship with alcohol. I used to be a big binge drinker in my late teens, and in my mid-twenties I was out every single night and got into trouble with some idiotic characters. But I'd always been afraid of that side of me for many years, as it only took one that might go down a little too well and I'd be off again. With the sun beating down across my shoulders I was sinking these with little restraint. I've always detested public speaking and was about to be standing in front of lots of my peers, and many television idols of mine, so it was quite nerve wracking.

Anyway Lee Bamber was the MC for this ceremony, and a cracking job he did of it too, after a good 45 minutes of awards and speeches from proud men and women all hobbling up to the microphone trying their best to hide their aged bones it was my time.

Lee said "The next award goes to a man who is very imposing. When you're up against him it's easy to feel a little worried. Next month he steps into the ring for the very last time after a fantastic career of twenty five years. A lot of youngsters have learnt a lot from this man who in the ring is quite frankly a Beast, a British Beast known as The Dominator. It's a lifetime achievement award for Stu Allen."

It was a cracking intro and it was then that I realised I'd not thought about what I was going to say. I'd planned fuck all. I wasn't pissed, but having listened to all the other old retired professionals telling their stories, you can imagine that these old guys and girls hadn't had a microphone in their hand for quite some time, let alone an audience, so were more than happy to be heard, and there was my stupid arse drinking in the hot sun like it was going out of fashion.

So here I was, handed the microphone, no script, and a good "beer buzz" on the go, as Sheryl Crowe calls it.

"I was a bit anxious about going to the gents before this speech ladies and gentlemen, but it's ok, I've just been informed that Kendo Nagasaki isn't here today."

Yes, a good old gay joke to get them going, that's definitely what was needed here.

I had a bit of a pop at old Sanjay Bagga, there in his best suit from Aldi, and his infamous paying of the boys in sandwiches. Probably completely uncalled for, but like Adam Sandler said in the Wedding Singer "I've got the microphone and you will listen!!"

I finished off by telling them what a task master that Adrian Street was and how the future of the business was in very good hands with likeminded students of the game who have old school values, certainly as far as my Academy was concerned anyway.

I signed off by saying what an honour it was to be standing before people who I'd idolised on television and thanked the Reunion for their very kind award. That was it, all over with.

I thought standing there waxing lyrical after a 25-year career compared to some who'd been doing it double that would be slightly absurd, so I made them laugh and got the fuck out of there. It seemed the right thing to do.

I have a couple of dozen wrestling posters I managed to get from around Europe where I had been top of the bill framed across our hallway at home. Also up there now is this special award which I'm extremely proud of. Tarn fucking hates all of them plastered everywhere, and I grant you, it's heavy on the eye, but they represent me doing stuff I never dreamt I'd have done in my life a couple of decades ago, not only that, but I have an irrational fear of large bare walls. So there.

The entire month was a bit of a whirlwind dominated by my looming retirement, the award, and now, as Monty Python used to say, "for something completely different". My wife waking me up early one Tuesday morning, the 10th of September to be exact, saying that she had something to tell me.
She sat on the bed and explained that she'd slept with someone else and that she was sorry, but I was going to hear it today and it had to be from her. It wasn't the "sleeping with" bit that upset me to be fair.

Now listen here dear reader, as jarring as that was, it's not half as jarring as this segue, but if something is going to rock you to your very foundations, and make you focus your mind on changing a few things, then that'll do it.
Everything went into slow motion. My heart dropped like a weight into my stomach and I was immediately shaken to my core. And although I didn't feel I deserved that, there was someone who deserved it even less than me in all of this. Not that that gave me any solace. But I hadn't been such a great husband in the fact that my addiction was starting to become the equivalent of the shadow of the UFO in Independence Day shadowing the city. From out of a few nights of fun, it had all of a sudden got a hold of me like nothing I'd ever experienced.

So I'm going to tell you something, and I need to write about this, as it's all part of the process. But this point in my life I remember very little, so it was a significant shift in my daily existence. I was a weekend offender, there's no two ways about it. An addict. Something I'd seen before as after all one of my very best friends had lived as one, but never did I ever expect that it would happen to me. But it did. And the mere thought of that admittance makes me go cold even now.

Addiction comes in many forms, sex, drugs, alcohol, food, gambling, social media, you name it. Our society is more geared up for addiction now more than ever, in fact it encourages it. I'll bet even after putting this very book down you'll scroll through your social media to see if that picture or status you posted has had a comment or like. It's instant gratification. Social media, whether we wish to admit it or not has made a lot of us dopamine junkies. It's legal, so it's fine yeah?? Just like alcohol. But honestly, it's as crippling in its own way.

I had always been unknowingly gripped by addiction all of my life in some form, whether it was excesses of food, booze, sex, cigarettes, there was always a fire burning deep inside me that could never be extinguished. A volume that I'd struggle to turn down every single waking moment of my life. Well I could turn it down, but never completely off, and it was always there, niggling away at me like the voice in my ear. The times I would be clean I'd be swept away in my sleep by overpowering dreams of scoring, and of course using, to such extent that I'd wake up exhausted and chewing my face off. Driving to places and passing old haunts where I'd been in some fuckers kitchen getting served or passing a dimly lit grubby corner where I'd meet my dealer making shit small talk whilst trying to keep the military operation of transference as slick as possible. It could never be one of anything, always too many even to the point where I'd just be doing whatever I wanted and people would be too afraid to tell me my behaviour was too much. But I honestly never saw it as a problem, and quite frankly, fuck blaming it on head traumas from car accidents or mental health disorders, addiction had been a large part of my life and only lay dormant occasionally. When it would rear up it was ugly and insatiable. I mean that in every single sense too, it would consume me so much that I wouldn't even feel sadness at the disappointment on my wife's face the next time I'd leave the house for another poor choice. As the saying goes, one is too much and ten is never enough.

After these bouts of hedonism I would just suffer with my depression for days after which was where the problem lay. It was a never-ending carousel of misery and self-torture that I was slowly pulling her into as well. The boil needed lancing. And

I'm not going to go into her reasons why she chose to do this, because that's not my story to tell, all I can do is give you my reasons why I wasn't always a good husband, its my book, my story, and I'm excusing nothing.

Thank god for getting clean and sober though. And actually, for the record, I must point out that god played no part in it, it was me – all me. If I can take the blame for getting in that shit in the first place then I'm not giving the big chap upstairs a pat on the back for getting me out of it.

Having found a wonderful sponsor and working a twelve-step programme I am able to live a normal life. It's funny, well, more embarrassing than funny actually. When I wrote my first book Simply the Beast, and indeed portions of this one, I've had to get a lot of information from people who were there on some of those shows with me because all of a sudden I realised that there was about a decade that I couldn't fucking remember. A whole portion of life I'd lived that was just completely leapfrogged, gone just like that. And that's pretty fucking awful when you consider how bloody short life is.

So yes, I did jump in my car, but not to drive off a fucking cliff. I went to buy a pack of cigarettes and called my work to let them know I wouldn't be coming in that day. I told my boss the reason. He told me not to do anything stupid, and I said I wouldn't, as I was speeding towards this piece of shits place of work to give him a morning surprise to match the one I'd just had.

Tarn and I met up late that night and went and sat on Galley hill in Bexhill with our beloved boy Milo and looked out to sea. It was a horrible day and she explained everything to me and was brutal in her honesty, but as much as I felt betrayed, I couldn't help but admire her accountability.

We knew that we loved each other in the strongest way possible. She proposed to me after three months of us being together and at this point had been married just over ten years. We'd been through a few very difficult times that would've broken most relationships, but right now, I trusted her. I know that there were more than a few people who would've rubbed their hands together at the thought of us cracking. People love a bit of dirty laundry don't they. But they weren't going to have their fun at our expense because we're not only above that but here I am choosing to

127

write about it for you to read about. There are no stones left unturned in my world. Whatever may happen, and in whatever direction life may take us, we shall remain unbreakable and unapologetic. Sorry people.

So of course it doesn't take a genius to figure out that the month of September wasn't the most ideal few weeks to build towards my final hurrah. I stopped eating, albeit not for long enough as I looked like a fat piece of shit on my retirement night. My mental health was all over the place and I did nothing in the gym at all. I had all these grand ideas of getting in great shape for one last go, but now I felt like I was pissing up a rope.

The final match would be held at our annual Halloween tradition Invasion of the Bodyslammers 9, inside the same structure that the Dominator arrived in back in 1998, the 15 foot high steel cage.
It was a tag team match, me and Skarlett against my old tag partner Titan and the EWW champ, Cyrus Shade.
The build to the match was a big one, done over the space of a couple of months with interviews on internet wrestling radio shows and local news sites including a lovely piece done by my friend at Hastings in Focus Stuart Baillie, who was doing a documentary about my final night.
It was a very surreal time for me all of this. What should've been a big proud moment for me was one now that I just wanted to get over and done with, and that is something that hurts me because all I did for Tarn since I met her was to build her up and make her the best that I possibly could, and yet here I was now only a fortnight away from my swansong and had been betrayed by the only person I'd ever been faithful and devoted to. It fucking stung that did. And rather than going out there all guns blazing and saying "Fuck the world, I'm gonna show all of you", instead I went into myself and was paranoid that everyone was there out of pity for me, because everyone must've known and everyone must've been talking about it. Look at that daft old cunt up there pretending he's still got it. My gun powder had

been well and truly dampened and I felt tired, my mind bulging with bad thoughts and intentions and scenarios that probably weren't even real. I have no idea.

All I do know is that this was no fucking Rocky montage before my final farewell, more of a dementia patient shuffle. The shit house shuffle.

Thanks everyone, just what I wanted.

CHAPTER TEN
THE FINAL CURTAIN

So here we were. Our biggest venue that we ever did at Extreme World Wrestling, the Sussex Coast College, this huge sprawling venue with five storied balconies high into the sky looking down onto our beautiful set up for the night. Lights, camera, action. Let's do it.

We knew we'd sold an unprecedented number of tickets and that this was going to be a very loud crowd indeed. Once again I'd famously overbooked the fucking card as so many people wanted to be on the card for my last night and I'd acquiesced to pretty much everybody, so it was going to be the full three hour extravaganza.

The difficulty we had with this show was getting the cage up in rapid time before the main event.

After a long show and an interval if you spend too long on getting a cage up you're asking for trouble. So we had time trials with our team during the day with Tarn screaming at the top of her lungs like a drill sergeant.

The first dummy run they got the cage up in twenty-two minutes. Not fucking good enough.

The second time, thirteen minutes. Still, not good enough.

The last time they go it up in seven minutes. The entire structure. It was absolutely brilliant. I said, yes, that's a bit more like it.

Listen I'm going to go straight into the match ok because I'll be perfectly frank with you, this night for me was fucking spoilt before it even began. I had all of my mates and students there backstage, and I sat there in silence trying to draw energy from anywhere to be able to get my game face on. But it wasn't coming. Now if you're reading this and thinking that I was feeling sorry for myself, you'd be missing the point all together. I'd been clean and sober for a short while and now not only was I fighting all of my preshow urges, but I was for the very first time in my wrestling career looking around me doubting those once trusting faces. My faith in people had been smashed to fucking smithereens and I'd never felt so fucking alone. I drew my outline of my warpaint on in the mirror as I had done over a thousand times and slowly used my tiny brush to sharpen the outline. I felt nothing. Nothing at all. Not nervous, not excited. Nothing.

People have always left me alone when I'm putting my warpaint on. That is when the ritual normally begins for me to slowly transform. It sounds daft perhaps if you've not performed in front of big crowds. But it's no different from Serena Williams bouncing the ball a certain amount of times before a serve or Steven Gerrard slapping the 'This is Anfield' sign before a game. It's ritual. And to some of us, it's crucial.

I chose my favourite wet look outfit for this one along with my classic latex spiked skull shoulder pads, and it was off to the races.

The match was an elimination chamber style match with the first two drawn together in the cage, Skarlett and Cyrus Shade.

Tarn had opted to get some new gear made by the wonderful Busty Keegan and it would emulate my own outfit, wet look black and red flames, she also wanted to use a little face-paint as homage to me and she'd made a drastic and somewhat Brtiney Spears-esque decision (without added breakdown I hasten to add) and shaved the left side of her head to the temple and had added a cobweb design shaved in there by our dear friend Jon Franklyn of Smooth Operators. It was a remarkable look, she looked like a cross between Luna Vachon and something off Mad Max with this huge mane of red hair and bright red grin, she looked great, she knew she had to stand aside for me tonight, but she also had a lot to prove and needed to dig deep.

She went into the cage and met her old rival Cyrus Shade face to face for the first time since he'd beaten her for the title. The opening exchanges were unbelievable, there's little point in starting a grudge match with anything other than a big jump start and both of them launched into each other with a flurry of punches and forearms, trading one for the other and knocking the shit out of each other. It was awesome. Obviously I was well out of sight at this point but could hear the audience rise up, and hear the breathe collectively leave their bodies as Skarlett would get brutally cut off. The particular bit of action that caused the huge gasp was when Cyrus caught her with a super kick, POW, right on the mark it was too. In typical Skarlett style she shook it off and came back with even more fire, she loves getting a wallop in the wrestling ring it gives her a phenomenal adrenaline rush, not to mention Carte-Blanche to give some back.

Then something unbelievable happened that could well have derailed the entire match. Cyrus was sitting on the top rope, intercepted by Tarn who came in to give him a superplex off the top. As she took off in mid-air, the turnbuckle literally snapped in half, it sounded like a pistol going off, and the top rope dropped. Thanks to Tarns strength she turned Cyrus in mid-air and prevented what would have almost certainly been a broken neck, it was remarkable. Luke Douton who had done the ring job ran out and was examining it from outside the cage although there was fuck all the daft sod could do as it was completely snapped in half. Having watched the replay it was as close to a wrestling tragedy as I've ever seen but was saved in the nick of time by strength and speed of mind by Tarnya.

With the top rope now gone and both wrestlers lying centre of the ring it was time for the next entrant. Three minutes had elapsed and the countdown clock started, who would be the wrestler who drew number three? Well of course it wasn't me, don't be so fucking stupid.

So here he came, striding down the ramp, Titan, stopping only to point at the cage and laugh to mock the fact that Skarlett was now well and truly out numbered.

Big Jonk and Tarn had never been in the ring together and the ridiculous size differential was a fantastic visual for the crowd. She fought back and every time she fought back there was a giant forearm to smash her back down to the ground again. He was toying with her, cat and mouse style. That was until she caught him off balance as he was steaming in to launch another attack and caught him with a stunning powerslam with such speed and use of momentum that at one point both of them were in mid-air. It was met with shrieks and gasps and rousing applause from the crowd.

I was now placed behind the curtain and I heard the thundering slam and the crowd come alive and that sent the hair on the back of my neck on end. Finally, the light came on in my head and it was time.

The countdown began and my old friend Chris O Regan, the man who'd been with us since our very first show in December of 1998 after answering an advert we put in The Stage magazine for a referee (baffling how things were before the internet), was the special guest MC and had travelled down from Lincolnshire to announce me for one last time, just as he had done for the very first time as The Dominator back in Oxford 25 years ago.

Stuart Baillie, a local journalist and his son who were documenting my retirement for a documentary were there behind me as Static-X's "Push It" hit the speakers and the place was thumping. I came through the curtain followed by the documentary camera crew, who I completely forgot were there in the fucking first place. I didn't look left or right, I took my shoulder pads straight off and launched them up and over the cage into the ring from some distance, something I'd never done before, I'd worn them into battle since Dominator started, but they went sailing through the air, over the top of the cage and into the ring, it was a great shot.

Someone opened the cage door and I went to step into the ring and realised there was no top rope. What the fuck had happened here? Nobody had come to the back to tell me anything, presumably so I wouldn't lose my fucking temper. But here I was climbing into chaos. It seemed that the world was standing still and the other three in the ring were frozen until I set foot in there.

I specifically remember walking down the aisle, unaware of people either side of me, complete and utter tunnel vision, and all three in the ring looking at me in their different positions. It was only as I went to climb in the ring that I realised there were only the two ropes left, before I had the chance to say "What the fuck has happened here you clumsy bunch of cunts" Cyrus was already flying off the middle rope into my choke slam, which he took like a hot bag of shit and we were away. He'd said "Don't worry Stu I'll fucking fly for you mate" Well, all I'll say is he forgot or he's a convincing liar because he left his flying boots at home that night and sandbagged me. I remember thinking straight away "Well this is all going well."

I launched him like a rag doll from one side of the cage to the other. Every time I went to pin him, Titan would leap in and break the count. Tarn leapt from the cage with a flying dropkick and the ring was strewn with humanity.

Cyrus was first to his feet and was making his way like the cowardly weasel he was out and over the top. Skarlett gave chase and the two of them were balanced precariously on the top exchanging shots, before both dangling over the other side swinging kicks at each others mid-section before dropping to the ground and fighting to the back, leaving just me and Titan alone in the ring for the big finale.

The leader of the Unknown, Trevor Bekooy was climbing the cage to help his lad out as I came steaming across and gave him a straight right to the mouth sending him plunging to the floor. Bondy, who is the despicable Trev Bekooy, said afterwards he could see the delight in my eyes as I ran towards him punching him in the mouth. I told him to shut the fuck up because it was gently cushioned by the fencing around the cage. He hasn't felt the fury of my straight right, and I consoled him by telling him that there was plenty of time for that.

Jonk and I turned to face each other and the fans realised that this was it, the moment the two monsters and former tag team partners were now one on one in the cage. We circled each other like caged animals soaking up the atmosphere before eventually locking horns.

Now I don't remember too much at this point as after letting Jonk beat me about he took his size twelves to the back of my head. The first one was fine, second one was lights out. Well, you think you're awake, and you feel like you're stretching your eyes wide open, but there's nothing and you hear ringing. It was only a very, very short time but it cleaned my clock. I'd done it to him enough times so I guess I was owed one.

Anyway, the finish was a belter I'd stolen from the great Dusty Rhodes. There was a chair in the centre of the ring. He bent down to grab it, and as he did so I stood on it. As he realised it's not moving he looks at me, I look out to the crowd, hook him and DDT him head first onto the chair. Only we did it way better than Lex and Dusty as Jonk spiked himself right on the chair and it looked fucking awesome. Eventually I draped one arm onto his chest and the referee counted to three. The place went off

135

and it was over. My wrestling career finished in what seemed the blink of an eye. If you're reading this and you're in the middle of yours, fucking enjoy every minute, because it's gone way, way quicker than you ever think possible.

Jonk and I both lay there. Over the noise I could hear him say "Bruv, bruv, look straight up".

I said "I already am mate" I was looking straight ahead all the way up to the high glass dome on top of the venue and Jonk and I were illuminated perfectly laying on our backs as if we were in the sky. It was surreal and quite a fitting end. Red streamers came shooting in from the balconies as I slowly rose to my feet and lay across the top of the cage and in the ring. I knew my dear old mum was up in the balcony somewhere watching and I knew that although she hated the wrestling she would understand this moment. Everyone on their feet and me stood in the middle of the cage, it honestly didn't feel real at all. What had been a roller-coaster couple of months had now come down to this, and I was proud, but also embarrassed if I'm honest. Getting praised or accolades doesn't come easy to us English folk, most of us naturally don't know how to contend with it, and this was the very end of the road for me with my peers and friends and fans giving me a rousing send off. Tarn did a speech on the mic, she's comfortable with that, and they all left me standing there. I thought to myself, "What happens here? Am I going to be waving like an idiot all night or will they eventually stop clapping and I'll just shuffle off in silence?" I just wanted a cup of tea, to watch Match of the Day and go to sleep. Worlds away from the post show nights of getting hammered, punching people and going to bed just as the birds start singing. Fuck all of that. It was time to go home.

It was several months later that an old friend of mine got in touch with me to discuss a reunion that I just couldn't resist. After 26 years I'd be seeing my dear wrestling coach again, 'Exotic' Adrian Street and Miss Linda.

Gary Van-Der Horne, an old friend of mine and promoter of Lucha Britannia in London, had organised 'An Audience with Adrian Street' at his venue the Resistance Gallery in Bethnal Green and asked if I wanted to be put on the guest list, so of course I couldn't refuse.

Adrian had moved back to his hometown of Wales to be closer to his family after beating throat cancer and had just been the subject of a WWE documentary called "Imagine What I Could Do To You" with clips from his career and sound-bites from a crop of current talent who had been inspired by him in some way.

I went up there with Tarnya and two of my trainees Bondy and Mary. As I walked through the dark entrance into the tiny venue I was greeted by Miss Linda who shouted "My handsome boy" and ran down the stairs and cupped my face in her hands so we were nose to nose, smiling and hugging. It was so wonderful to see her. I love Linda so much she's an absolute angel of a woman and so warm and not to mention tough as they come.

And just as we started talking about old times here came the man himself down the stairs, pausing only to appear god like above us all - Adrian.

"Sadie!!" He shouted. It was lovely for my students to meet the man who is essentially their wrestling grandfather. And of course, Adrian refused to get off the bottom two steps so he was taller than me in our picture together. Ever the show man. It was wonderful to catch up with him and to be able to introduce him to three of my own wrestling students. Both Adrian and Linda were fans of Skarlett and Adrian even wrote about how good he thought she was in his autobiography. His seventh volume in fact. Don't worry, I managed to squeeze mine into just the two...

It was a cracking evening packed full of Adrian's stories, most of which I'd heard on a daily basis, normally whilst being tortured in a variety of holds I didn't know how to escape from, but it was a pleasure to revisit them all over again with he and Linda sat on the stage, and Linda staring adoringly at him even after all these years. It was so beautiful.

Tarn sat with me in the front row and Adrian would keep looking over to me after each story to see if I was laughing, and in turn he'd start laughing, it was like going back to 1994.

I was sat next to Paul Tyrell, who was the only other English man to graduate Skullkrushers, along with Bernard Van Damme who was a great worker from

Belgium. Adrian sang the praises of all three of us and said that Paul and I were his favourite students to teach.

He did a good hour and then it was a Q and A from the audience, and it was time to go. It was an emotional evening seeing Adrian and Linda after my retirement. The last time I'd seen them I was heading off in a car for Miami, driving through the night on my way home to try and carve out a career as a professional wrestler after so many scoffed or said I was too small, or that I was wasting my time.

I often wonder what would've become of me if I had listened to them. I'd have had to have done something unusual, I was never cut out to be an office bod or a labourer. Not ever.

Even when I was at my lowest, and fresh out of hospital in baggy dirty clothes, walking through Tilgate Forest with my old mate Jonk, we were stopped by two elderly women who said, "You're both wrestlers aren't you?"

As it turned out, we were. But she hadn't recognised us. She simply knew. And how specific. We were both looking scruffy as fuck, and they knew we were something. Could've said rugby players or door men, but no, wrestlers was what she said. And how many British wrestlers nowadays can have that effect on people, to be able to feel like they can approach you and instinctively know what it is they do? Not many, I can assure you. So I guess it was meant to be. And as much as they drive me nuts, some of my old wrestling compadres and my students who sometimes leave me incandescent with rage, I wouldn't be without them. They keep me going, they keep me young, and they keep me vital. And as for wrestling, it's a constant that will always be there, and that's very comforting to know.

It's a wonderful world of make believe to get lost in and having been in it for nearly three decades in varying degrees of success, I still enjoy watching it and learning. I appreciate everyone who steps between the ropes to entertain, and I still believe it to be one of the greatest and most underappreciated art forms of them all. We are entertainers, but we are also athletes, story tellers and stunt people, and we do it all in one take.

You really can't top that.

FURTHER INFORMATION

EWW Wrestling – eww-wrestling.com

Extreme Academy of Wrestling –
Search Extreme Academy of Wrestling on Facebook

Stiff Right Hand Podcast – www.stiffrighthand.com

ABOUT THE AUTHORS

Stu Allen is a veteran of the British Wrestling industry having been a wrestler and promoter for nearly 30 years. He has wrestled in countries all over the world and is the founder of the highly acclaimed promotion Extreme World Wrestling, and Head Teacher of the Extreme Academy of Wrestling. Stu also created and presents the Stiff Right Hand podcast and his previous autobiography 'Simply The Beast' was released in 2020.

Neil Cameron lives in Suffolk and has worked in the travel and events industry for over two decades. He has written for numerous publications and has published the books *'Through the Shattered Glass'*, *'Wrestling with my Mind'* and *'Simply The Beast'*.

Printed in Great Britain
by Amazon

46023785R00086